T0269926

AN IDENTIFICATION GUIDE TO
GARDEN BIRDS
OF **BRITAIN**
and North-West Europe

Dominic Couzens
and Carl Bovis

JOHN BEAUFOY PUBLISHING

First published in the United Kingdom in 2023 by John Beaufoy Publishing Ltd
11 Blenheim Court, 316 Woodstock Road, Oxford OX2 7NS, England
www.johnbeaufoy.com

Copyright © 2023 John Beaufoy Publishing Ltd
Copyright in text © 2023 Dominic Couzens and Carl Bovis
Copyright in photographs © 2023 Carl Bovis, except as specified below
Copyright in maps © 2023 John Beaufoy Publishing Ltd

Photo Credits
Front cover: Robin © Carl Bovis
Back cover, top to bottom: Blue Tit; Goldfinch; Kestrel, all © Carl Bovis
Spine: Song Thrush © Carl Bovis

All other photographs by Carl Bovis except:
Allan Chard p.51. Bob Gibbons p.36, p.37, p.42, p.43, p.44, p.45 bottom, p.60,
p.61 top, p.72 top & bottom, p.73, p.128, p.129 top & bottom, p.150. Pixabay/
sarangib p.53. Amano Samarpan p.61 bottom, p.101, p.151 top & bottom, p.152
left, p.153. Shutterstock/Piotr Krzeslak p.19; Julie Gaia p.46; Ihor Hvozdetskyi
p.50, p.100; Ronald Wittek p.52; Marek Cech p.78; Nick Vorobey p.79; Martin
Pelanek p.94, Hannu Rama p.105; RazvanZinica p.117; stmilan p.124 right;
Sandra Standbridge p. 125.

All rights reserved. No part of this publication may be reproduced, stored
in a retrieval system or transmitted in any form or by any means, electronic,
mechanical, photocopying, recording or otherwise, without the prior written
permission of the publishers.

Great care has been taken to maintain the accuracy of the information
contained in this work. However, neither the publishers nor the authors can be
held responsible for any consequences arising from the use of the information
contained therein.

ISBN 978-1-913679-33-0

Edited and index by Krystyna Mayer
Designed by Nigel Partridge
Project management by Rosemary Wilkinson

Printed and bound in Malaysia by Times Offset (M) Sdn. Bhd.

CONTENTS

INTRODUCTION

This book is an introduction to the birds you might see in your garden, and a few that might fly over it. Most species that appear around houses in Britain and north-west Europe are included. Obviously, in such a large area, unusual species of all kinds can turn up, especially in rural or isolated locations – but most species that you may see in a garden are featured here.

The information provided should help you to identify the birds you might see, so photographs of them in their various guises have been included, as have tips about how to recognize each bird. Also included is key information enabling you to delve a little into the fascinating lives of the species covered – because they are amazing. There is information on the birds' lifestyles, including nesting, migration and feeding, as well as a range of additional facts about them. Garden birds, especially in Europe, are among the best studied in the world, and it is simply extraordinary to learn what some of them can get up to.

Another aim of the book is to make garden birdwatching fun. That is why some well-known and unusual photographs by Carl Bovis, which often appear online (p. 158), have been included. Birds are beautiful, entertaining, fascinating and an enormous delight in life, and watching them is a marvellous tonic for coping with our complex and sometimes difficult world. Garden birds are everyday birds, helping to lift our everyday lives.

The information provided here should enhance your love of birds and encourage you to help them. We all know that wild creatures around the world are under pressure from many human-induced problems, and they need our protection. Everyone can do something, and a garden or local shared space is a very good place to start.

IDENTIFYING GARDEN BIRDS

Welcome to the delightful challenge of identifying your avian visitors. We all know some birds – pigeons, crows and sparrows, for instance. The easiest way to use this book is simply to leaf through the photographs a few times and get an idea of what other birds could visit your neighbourhood. The more you look through the pages, the more birds you will begin to recognize. If you have not done so already, you will start noticing birds such as Blackbirds, Robins, Magpies and Goldfinches this way.

Identifying the birds in your garden or local space is different from going birdwatching. In a garden, you tend to see your visitors at a closer range, and for longer, and it is a lot easier to recognize a bird at a feeder or bird bath than it is to determine a speck out in an estuary or far away on a lake. You also have a narrower range of species to choose from. That is why gardens are great places in which to learn about and appreciate birds. The more you watch, the more you will notice, and you will find that you take in a great deal subconsciously, without really trying. You begin to form images in your mind of what birds look like, how large they are compared to each other, and so on. Your path to bird identification mastery can end here if you like.

However, you can go further in observing the birds in your garden. To do this you need to acquire a pair of binoculars, even just for the garden or neighbourhood. They can transform the garden-bird experience, working by magnifying an image so that you can appreciate details that would otherwise be impossible to see. This is really your key to the finer points – the speckles and spots, the wing-bars and the moustachial stripes are the so-called 'field marks' on a bird. It makes it easier to distinguish similar species, like the Song Thrush and Mistle Thrush, as well as to tell males, females and juveniles apart.

There is not the space here to provide information on the many types of binoculars available (and you can buy spotting scopes for birding, too). Go for an inexpensive but not bargain pair. It's a good idea to buy from a conservation organization such as the Royal Society for the Protection of Birds in the UK (see p. 158 for other organizations); many have web pages that provide advice. Specialist shops exist, and specialist magazines also have listings of sources. It is best to try out a pair of binoculars first. Go for comfort – this usually means obtaining a lightweight pair, which is perfectly adequate for a garden.

Once you have come to grips with binoculars, you can try the same process of learning by experience as you did without them. You will begin to notice the white nape mark on a Coal Tit and the grey rump of a Fieldfare. Again, the more birds you scan, the more you will pick up; your skills will grow naturally.

For the keenest, however, there is one more step you can take to raise your identification game, and that is to learn to look at birds critically. Unless you have a photographic memory, this will not come at all naturally. We humans are remarkably poor at noticing and remembering details. However, if you are methodical, you are on the way to being a very good birdwatcher.

The process is deceptively simple. You look at a bird and make sure you watch it long enough to take in as many details of its plumage as possible. You can begin at the head and work down to the tail, or vice versa – it does not matter. It is all a matter of practice. People sometimes train themselves by writing down these details in a personal notebook, just so they do not miss a detail. It can become a great record of your garden's birdlife.

Of course, you can bypass all this effort by taking photographs. The details are recorded in an instant, and most birds can be identified even with poor efforts.

If you wish to go down the methodical route, and also get the very best out of the descriptions in this book, it is helpful to learn about the different parts of a bird. The diagrams below show the physical features that are mentioned in the text.

There is yet one more thing to mention about bird identification using sight, and that is taking in the *character* of a bird. You will undoubtedly know people in your life who are obvious just from their manner – their shape, their movements and their idiosyncrasies. Birds are the same. Wagtails wag their tails, Starlings hustle and bustle, and Nuthatches hold on to tree trunks head down. Sometimes you hardly need to see the plumage to know what a bird is. As your experience grows, you will soon be able to identify birds by behaviour alone.

Bird Sounds Identifying bird songs and calls is an order of magnitude more difficult than sight recognition. Many people get quite frustrated by not knowing what they are listening to. However, with a little effort most people can make considerable headway.

Think of this. How many human voices do you think you can recognize – for example those of friends, family, work colleagues and acquaintances? There will be hundreds. Most people with satisfactory hearing ability can tell a myriad human voices from

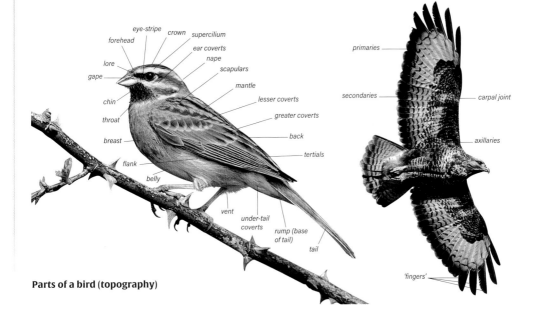

Parts of a bird (topography)

eye-stripe
forehead
crown
supercilium
ear coverts
nape
scapulars
lore
gape
mantle
chin
lesser coverts
throat
greater coverts
breast
back
flank
tertials
belly
vent
under-tail coverts
rump (base of tail)
tail

primaries
secondaries
carpal joint
axillaries
'fingers'

subtle auditory clues. It does not even matter if they are tone deaf – they can still do it. So, in theory, most people should be able to master a lot of bird sounds. The majority of bird sounds are right in the sweet spot of human hearing.

Many of us know some bird vocalizations – the *caw* of a crow, the quack of a duck and the *coo* of a dove, for example – and, of course, the voice of the Cuckoo. That is a starting platform. The advantage of gardens, meanwhile, is that there is only a limited number of species that are singing or calling. So a large number of all the sounds in your garden are made by a small range of species.

Having said that, there is no quick fix, because identifying an unseen voice without context is still very difficult. Here, every effort has been made to give memorable descriptions of calls and songs (included under the heading 'Voice'), and these will sometimes help. However, there is no substitute for trying to get a visual on a singing bird. Your mind will conflate the unfamiliar (the song or call) with the familiar (seeing the bird that is vocalizing) and it will become easier to recognize the bird, especially if you encounter the singer many times.

It was once quite difficult to acquire recorded bird sounds, but today there are plenty of websites that have everything you need. There are even apps that claim to identify bird sounds for you, and they often work. Also check out the many bird books available for descriptions of bird sounds and other identifying features (see Further Reading, p. 158).

LOOKING AFTER GARDEN BIRDS

There are two ways in which you can help birds thrive in the garden: you can help them either directly or indirectly. Direct help lies in the provision of feeding stations, where you can enjoy the birds lapping up the good things that you have provided, including food and water. Indirect help lies in providing good habitat for birds, by being smart and sympathetic to how your garden is designed.

While there is enormous benefit in direct help for birds, and a happy symbiosis when you, the garden owner, increase your delight in and regard for avian visitors as you watch their antics at close quarters,

arguably you can provide more benefit indirectly with garden management. It is easy to overlook this. For example, someone may find themselves cutting down a tree that they consider a nuisance, but at the same time put up a bird table. However, overall, it is probably better to spare the tree, especially if it is an old one. Or perhaps someone puts up a nest-box but gets rid of clumps of ivy; again, this is a net loss. Ivy is a fabulous plant for wildlife, providing hiding places for numerous creatures, some of which provide food for birds much more efficiently than any artificial feeder, and it also produces a marvellous crop of early spring berries. Moreover, ivy is a great plant in which birds can nest and find shelter.

This, then, is a plea for smart and forward-looking garden management. If you love birds, you will make a good environment for them in your garden. Wildlife needs all the help it can get, and conservation truly begins at home. You can provide an incredible amount of benefit at very low cost. The good thing is that often you can literally do this by some creative laziness.

A tidy garden looks good, but sterility is a disaster for wildlife. If gardeners wish to benefit birds, they need to embrace untidiness and imperfection. It is not that the garden needs to be a mess – it just needs to be a little more 'frayed at the edges'. First things first – avoid the monstrosity of a plastic lawn unless it is necessary for access. Secondly, try to leave some dead or dying wood in place; that does not necessarily mean keeping a dangerous tree upright, but why not make a woodpile from the logs? Thirdly, try to reconcile with plants going to seed, because they are often good habitat. Fourthly, why not keep the mowing down to the lowest level you can bear? A grass lawn is good, but a lawn studded with herbs is better.

Another offshoot of coping with untidiness is coping without pesticides or herbicides. Yes, of course you will not want aphids on your roses, but you know what? The birds will. Aphids are food. Equally, you might not want slugs or snails, but something will eat these for you. If you have to control 'pests' – and obviously, if you are a commercial grower you wish to make your profits –

do so organically if possible. However, the majority of gardeners could cope with at least some infestations of unwanted insects or weeds.

Besides leaving some untidiness, another favour you can do birds and insects is to be clever with your planting. Birds will benefit from berry-bearing shrubs, for example – especially, but not always, native ones. Bees and other insects will benefit from nectar-rich flowers. There is plenty of information out there to help you select good blooms, shrubs or trees – and remember to leave that ivy.

Feeding Stations Who does not want to watch birds come and go at the feeding stations they have provided? It is tremendous fun, and you help the birds, too. The sheer long-term entertainment is a great boost to many people.

There is masses of information out there about what to feed birds and what sort of feeders to buy. You can buy everything from a traditional tray bird table to a sort of apartment complex of hanging feeders. You can also purchase an extraordinary variety of foodstuffs aimed at different bird species.

Details of specific bird foods are not provided here except for some general advice that might be helpful, and good for the birds. The first thing to mention is

A male Blackcap and two Goldfinches at a feeder.

hygiene. There have been a number of outbreaks of diseases recently, mostly affecting Chaffinches and Greenfinches, and you will help to mitigate these by cleaning your feeders regularly, as often as once every two weeks. It is also suggested that you move feeders around. Most bird diseases are spread by droppings. Make sure that you have feeders that are easy to take down and clean.

Try to keep feeders regularly stocked up. This is simply because birds tend to have daily routines and this will help them.

The general hygiene of the garden will be helped if you use no-mess bird-feeding mixes, preventing the build-up of discarded seed husks. Also, it is best not to throw seed on to the grass, but have a ground tray station instead, as you can remove this at night to avoid being too generous to rats. Not long ago, people used to throw out kitchen scraps, but these days most of us buy selections of bird food online, from a supermarket or garden centre. In general, this is a better idea.

Do not forget to provide water, too. Use a special tray or bird bath. Most birds do not need much water, but you will get a lot of joy out of watching the antics at a bird bath.

Also do not worry about the fact that your feeders might attract predators such as Sparrowhawks. They are a fact of life and also, you might be surprised

to hear, a sign of a decent bird population. One last thing: try to be realistic in your expectations. A garden's bird list is only as good as its overall location. There are a lot of birds in this book, and no garden will have them all.

Nest-boxes Also known as 'bird houses', nest-boxes provide another way of helping garden birds, by supplying high-quality housing for the discerning bird. The only problem is that the birds themselves are notoriously choosy, and do not always nest where we think they should.

You do not need to provide nest-boxes – after all, cavity-nesting birds have managed for more than a million years without our help – but there is nothing quite like a pair of birds moving in and raising a family in the space we have provided. Nest-boxes can even be fitted with cameras so you can watch the birds' activities on a television or computer screen. It is good drama – often much better than a television programme. It is also a lot messier and earthier than we usually expect.

Siting a nest-box is not complicated. Just put it up on a tree and make sure it does not face south, in case it gets too much sun and overheats. Leave it alone and manage your expectations.

There are various designs of nest-box, and you can get many that are species specific: owl boxes, Swift boxes, and so on. Some have holes and others have open fronts, so make sure you put up the right box for the species you wish to attract. Do get nest-boxes from a reputable supplier, especially an ethical one. Avoid the more ornate designs, which usually have humans in mind rather than birds. That incidentally also applies to your feeders.

For the ultimate environmental satisfaction, why not make your own nest-box? If a pair of birds uses it, the buzz is quite something.

GARDEN BIRDS THROUGH THE YEAR

One of the many joys of garden birdwatching is that it is a year-round activity. In fact, when the gardening jobs wind down in winter, the bird activity can be most feverish. The lack of vegetation and colour is compensated for by the hustle and bustle at feeders – and this is the case right at the start of the year.

The New Year follows the winter solstice (usually 21 December), so by the time **January** comes around, the days are already lengthening. This is an important biological trigger, and its first effect is an increase in bird song. There is not much in the first weeks, but by the end of January the bird chorus is noticeable. Tits in particular, especially the Great Tit, can fill the neighbourhood with their cheerful songs. Other species begin, too, including the Coal Tit, Blue Tit, Nuthatch and Starling, making a great chatter on warm days. In rural areas, Rooks are already building nests and noisily attending their colonies, a sure sign of the breeding season ahead.

In **February** the dawn chorus, in the dark, may become ever more noticeable. Song Thrushes will have been singing since midwinter and, together with Robins and, now, Blackbirds, make a haunting soundtrack to the winter gloaming. Chaffinches also begin to sing. In Scandinavia, the first Starlings begin to appear from the south, signalling the inevitability of spring. Things are changing at the feeders, too, and in many gardens the number and variety of species is unrivalled. That is because, for much of the winter, the wider countryside, still offering the fruits of autumn in the form of stores of nuts and seeds, has sustained many birds, but these supplies are dwindling. More and more birds, wandering around, find garden stores.

Although the flowering of willows provides some new food in the form of blooms and their attendant insects, **March** is a tough month. Almost every resident bird should have a territory and males of our bird species are very busy with their songs, protecting their precious spaces. Females are getting in shape to produce eggs. At the same time, food can be very short – this is the so-called 'hunger gap' between autumn abundance and the surge in insects – so it is an important time to keep the feeding stations stocked up. Every resident bird is singing and a few species, such as the Mistle Thrush and Tawny Owl, are already well into their nesting cycles.

Several summer visitors arrive in March, with the first Swallows arriving on the Continent late in the month, along with Chiffchaffs. Further north, Redwings and Fieldfares, together with many other migrants, appear after their short-haul flights from Britain, France and southern Europe. However, **April** signals huge arrivals of everything else, from Blackcaps to Pied Flycatchers. These are settling in months for them. Meanwhile, most resident birds, such as Robins, tits, Carrion Crows and Dunnocks, build nests and incubate eggs during April. This is often a time when garden feeder use reduces a little.

The precious weeks of April and **May** are the breeding season for most European birds. The last arrivals are Swifts and Spotted Flycatchers, both of which catch insects in the hopefully warm spring air. If we think birds are busy, what about invertebrates? Simply billions of insects are hatching, providing food for birds and other animals. The sheer complexity of life, even in a modest garden or shared space, is astonishing. The weather in April and May tends to determine the success of the breeding season. Some rain is useful, but not too much, and plenty of sunshine is good. Wind and cold, with persistent rain, are bad news for most birds.

June sees something of a frenzy of reproduction. Depending on the latitude (everything starts later in the north of the region covered here), at least something will be nest building, or incubating eggs, or feeding nestlings, or pushing fledglings out into the big wide world. To birds it is frantic – to us it is fun to watch. Fluffy balls of juvenile birds, with cut-price plumage and clueless demeanour, find their way on to lawns and feeders, and their vulnerability is frightening. The losses at all breeding stages are enormous, but it has always been this way.

It is remarkable how quickly the breeding season winds down. Once again, the first clue is the fall in bird song, and even by mid-May many birds, such as Great Tits, have stopped singing. The end of June becomes very quiet. However, in July there can be a brief resurgence, as birds such as Song Thrushes move on to a second brood. The finches are a gift that never stops giving; Greenfinches and Goldfinches carry on breeding right to the end of summer, and are busy and lively.

In **July**, many birds are moulting and subdued; changing the feathers requires a lot of energy, so birds become quiet and inactive. In midsummer, many juvenile birds, such as Starlings, gather into flocks; tits may form roaming parties, often attracting various other birds, such as warblers or Goldcrests, to join them. In late summer, in July and **August**, pigeons often provide rich entertainment, cooing noisily from rooftops and indulging in their pleasing flight displays.

September is a month of change and shifting. Most birds have completed their moult and the bird population consists of adults and the new batch of juveniles. Many bird species become more sociable. Others, including tits, begin to change their diet from a largely insectivorous one to one of seeds. Everywhere, berries become important, and this is a time when you will be grateful for any berry-bearing tree or shrub you planted in the garden. Berries fuel migratory flights for many birds, and the great southward migration has begun. Swallows gathering excitedly on wires are a classic symbol of migration.

October sees the same shifts. By the middle of this month, most transcontinental migrants such as Swallows and warblers have left Europe until the next spring. However, it is also a month of arrivals, as millions of birds make smaller migratory shifts. For example, vast numbers of birds such as Blackbirds, Black-headed Gulls, Starlings and wagtails make their way from Scandinavia and the edge of the Baltic to the more temperate parts of the region, and from highlands to lowlands. These movements involve garden birds as much as any others.

The movements continue throughout **November**. This can be a quiet month on the garden feeders, as most birds concentrate on the bounty of berries, nuts and seeds in the countryside at large. By now, due to the rapidly dwindling daylight, birds settle into their winter pattern of all-day feeding and finding a safe place to roost. A few birds, such as Robins and Wrens, sing to defend their winter territories.

December sees few movements as the days become so short, and the weather so unkind, that survival is the only aim for most species. The key to staying alive is in getting enough food. Garden birdfeeders thus provide a lifeline for many birds.

GLOSSARY

advertising call Equivalent of song given by birds other than songbirds, used to declare ownership of a territory and willingness to pair up.

breeding Term used for the whole reproductive cycle, from pairing up to producing young.

brood Collection of young constituting a single breeding attempt.

brooding When an adult sits on young birds to keep them warm, the equivalent of incubating eggs.

call Broadly, any vocalization that is not used as a **song**. It includes alarm calls, contact calls and calls to a mate. It is not a specific scientific term.

colony Clearly defined gathering of pairs for breeding, each pair with its own nest and a small territory around the nest.

crop A muscular pouch behind the mouth where birds can store food prior to digestion.

cryptic Refers to colouration or patterning for concealment.

dabbling Act of a bird placing the bill in water to feed, usually at the surface.

display Set of postures and movements designed to threaten or attract another bird, often for courtship.

display flight Aerial display, usually with a territorial function.

down Small feathers characterized by their fluffy structure.

dust bathing Form of bathing in earth or soil. Helps to remove parasites, oils and detritus.

fledging Act of acquiring first set of juvenile feathers, a prerequisite to leaving nest.

fledgling Bird that has fledged and left nest.

invertebrate General term for vast assemblage of animals without backbones, including insects, spiders, crustaceans, worms, and so on.

juvenile Bird sporting its first set of feathers.

migration Regular movement, usually seasonal, between one place and another, undertaken by a species or population.

nest Structure made for containing eggs and young and keeping them together.

nestling Young bird confined, owing to its stage of development, to nest.

omnivore Refers to bird (or other animal) that will eat anything, including animal and vegetable material.

plumage Current set of feathers covering a bird. Often differs between male, female and juvenile, and sometimes from one season to another.

raptor General term for day-flying bird of prey.

resident Refers to bird that lives in the same place, both very specific and more general (for example a country), throughout the year.

roost Site used for resting, usually at night, by one or many individuals.

roosting Preparing and going to sleep.

sedentary Refers to bird that does not migrate.

song Pattern of sounds, used to proclaim territorial ownership of a place, and/or to attract a mate. Often heard only during specific seasons.

species Group of organisms reproductively isolated from other such groups, and capable of interbreeding and producing fertile young.

territory Area defended by a bird for breeding or feeding purposes, or both.

NOTES ON SPECIES DESCRIPTIONS

The months highlighted in the calendar at the top of the page are a guide to when the species might be seen (in Britain). The maps show all-year-round presence in green, summer residence in orange and wintering (non-breeding) areas in blue.

 An introduction to the species. Calls and songs are grouped together under 'Voice'.

 The breeding of the species. Relevant notes are included, but are not exhaustive.

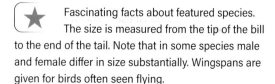 Fascinating facts about featured species. The size is measured from the tip of the bill to the end of the tail. Note that in some species male and female differ in size substantially. Wingspans are given for birds often seen flying.

The area covered includes Britain, Ireland, northern France, Belgium, the Netherlands, Luxembourg, northern Germany, northern Poland, the Baltic States, Scandinavia, Finland and Iceland.

| JAN | FEB | MAR | APR | MAY | JUN | JUL | AUG | SEP | OCT | NOV | DEC |

CANADA GOOSE

Branta canadensis

This is a bird to see from the garden rather than in it. Flocks often commute noisily overhead, at rooftop height. It is familiar from park lakes and other wetlands, where it is far from shy and retiring. It is at home in the water, where it sometimes feeds with neck submerged and tail up (up-ending). It spends much time grazing on grass and loafing about, enlivening the day with regular bickering.

This is a big bird, almost the size of a swan, with a very long neck. It is graceful in flight, where flock members form ragged lines as well as 'V' formations. **ADULT** Unremarkable except for black head and neck with a stark white chin. **JUVENILE** The yellow goslings are attractive, but soon grow into gangling, dishevelled adolescents, with dull rather than white chin markings. **VOICE** A variety of grating, trumpeting calls with two settings: loud and very loud. **MIGRATION** Does not usually move far except in Scandinavia, where populations fly south in winter.

BREEDING April–June, one brood. **NEST** Hollow lined with vegetation and down, usually on an island in a lake, but otherwise close to water. **EGGS** 5–6, incubated by female for about a month. **YOUNG** Can quickly run about and swim after hatching; fly at 60 plus days.

Canada Geese sometimes form 'gang broods', where two or more families and their young spend all their time together.

Introduced to Europe from North America (Britain 17th century, Continent 20th). Locally common near large waterbodies.

white chin-strap

FACT FILE

FAMILY Anatidae (Wildfowl). **SIZE** Length 80–110cm. Wingspan 155–180cm. **FOOD** Eats grass and other plant material and defecates with notable regularity (every few minutes). **SIMILAR SPECIES** The Greylag Goose (*Anser anser*) lacks the black neck and white chinstrap.

MALLARD

Anas platyrhynchos

Generally abundant in any freshwater habitat, but scarcer in the north.

When people think of a duck, it is almost invariably the Mallard. It is the most abundant duck in the wild, in park lakes and on the dinner table. Large gardens with ponds may attract Mallards to breed, and they are so common that they will fly over any garden or shared space at some time. Many people's earliest experiences of wild birds concern ducks coming for food at ponds, where they famously bicker and quack (the ducks, that is). They have a remarkably diverse range of feeding techniques and foodstuff, from 'dabbling' (putting the bill to the surface of the water) to gripping vegetation and up-ending to catch animals such as snails. However, they do not usually dive under the surface.

Mallards are relatively large ducks, with a fast and powerful flight, and whistling wingbeats. They have big, flattened bills that help them dabble and filter food. Due to a long period of domestication, various breeds have arisen, which readily enter the wild population and do what ducks do, resulting in many individuals with odd patterns, colours and shapes. **MALE** Handsome, with a gorgeous, beer-bottle green sheen on the head and neck, as well as a smart yellow bill. Note the manicured up-curled tail feathers, a sort of midlife-crisis afterthought, also visible in flight. Note that many ex-domestic Mallards look quite

bottle-green head

yellow bill

LEFT: *FEMALE*

BELOW: *MALE IN FLIGHT (NOTE PURPLE SPECULUM WITH WHITE EDGES)*

different, and may even be pure white. **FEMALE** Very different from male – streaky-brown, with variations in ground colour. The bill is large and there is an obvious stripe through the eye. Note that in summer (June–August) males moult and look very similar to females, apart from the yellow bill. Both sexes have a special feature on the wing, visible in flight and seen on many ducks, called the speculum. In Mallards it is purple, bordered on both sides with white. **VOICE** Familiar quack – the loud volleys of quacks, with the ring of a belly laugh, are made by females. In display the males utter a curious, somewhat feeble whistle and quiet quack. **MIGRATION** Northern and eastern populations fly south in the winter, in October–March.

 BREEDING March–July, one brood. **NEST** Secreted within thick herbage, this is a shallow hollow on the ground, lined with leaves and the female's own down feathers, which are used to conceal the eggs when the female is absent. **EGGS** 10–12, incubated by female (in absence of male) for 28–29 days. **YOUNG** Hatch as ready-made fluffballs that can soon follow the mother to water; they fledge at 7–8 weeks.

★ In contrast to most other birds, ducks have penises.

FACT FILE

FAMILY Anatidae (Wildfowl). SIZE Length 50–60cm. Wingspan 81–95cm. FOOD Omnivore, taking everything from midges (in summer) to grain. SIMILAR SPECIES There are many duck species, but few are likely to be found in any but the largest gardens.

GREY HERON

Ardea cinerea

Locally common in freshwater habitats including ponds, lakes and large rivers.

This is not a typical garden bird, but it does have a predilection for ponds and the fish in them. It is entirely unmistakable, being the only tall, long-legged bird likely to suss out your pond, which it will probably do in the early morning. Its patient hunting method involves standing still, usually with its feet in the water, waiting for a fish or frog to come within range, then to strike at it with a grab of the bill. Herons spend much time standing still and they often retract the neck and appear to raise their shoulders, like a person caught in a downpour lifting the collar of a raincoat. They also assume a wild-eyed look that can appear hilariously fed up.

The birds are tall, with a long neck and long legs. They look grey. In flight, the neck is retracted, the feet very obviously trail behind, and they fly with slow, heavy wingbeats on broad wings. **ADULT** White head

FACT FILE

FAMILY Ardeidae (Herons). SIZE Length 84–102cm. Wingspan 155–175cm. FOOD Fish (often quite large), frogs, young birds, small mammals including moles. SIMILAR SPECIES The White Stork (*Ciconia ciconia*) is a common garden and roadside bird in southern Europe and a few parts of the region. It has black-and-white plumage and a red bill, and flies, unlike the heron, with neck extended.

black plume on
whitish head

with black stripe through eye. Stripe becomes a plume. **JUVENILE** Grey
crown and no black plume. **MIGRATION** Largely resident, although
some Scandinavian birds move south in winter.

BELOW: *JUVENILE*

BREEDING Very early, refurbishing nests in
February, and laying eggs in March; some
young are still in the nest in June. **NEST** Large platform
of sticks, perhaps where you would least expect it – in
the treetops. Colonial. **EGGS** 3–4, incubated for 23–28
days. **YOUNG** Leave nest from six weeks old.

A study in England on non-breeding
individuals found that, for 77 per cent of their
day, they simply did nothing at all – not sleeping (6 per
cent), preening or feeding – nothing!

Herons do not impale the fish they catch
– they just grab them. They have specially
adapted neck vertebrae for snapping towards prey.

Common in lowland rural areas.

| JAN | FEB | MAR | APR | MAY | JUN | JUL | AUG | SEP | OCT | NOV | DEC |

PHEASANT

Phasianus colchicus

This is a bird you would only expect to find in rural gardens, possibly as a refugee from a shoot. It does, however, become quite tame and readily beds in as a client of feeding stations, especially at ground level. The male is completely unmistakable, covered with opulent feathered bling. It is stunning and knows it, strutting around with an air of 'I know I'm beautiful'. It often ruffles its feathers and lifts its tail, making no attempt at concealment. The female is also distinctive, with a long, pointy tail, but just less exaggerated and more furtive. The Pheasant is quite reluctant to fly, and if you disturb it or come across it on a country road, it prefers to run away, even if this does not seem like the smart thing to do.

This is a large, familiar game bird with a long tail and regal air. That is until it flies, which it does with a sudden take-off and a slightly desperate-looking flapping of its rounded wings. **MALE** Unmistakable opulent beauty with long train for a tail. Some males have a white neck-ring, others do not. There are colour varieties, including white and green birds. **FEMALE** Dressed for cryptic camouflage, but still with long tail-spike. **JUVENILE** Lacks much of a tail, so a little confusing.

some males have white neck-ring

VOICE Loud, double cough, quite hoarse. In spring, male combines it with wing-flapping. Also coughs in series in alarm. **MIGRATION** Not a migrant.

 BREEDING March–June, when 2–3 females form a small, exclusive harem around a chosen male. **NEST** Shallow hollow under cover of thick, weedy vegetation, in male's territory. **EGGS** 7–15, incubated by female (male plays little or no part) for 23–28 days. **YOUNG** After hatching, young can immediately run about and feed themselves. They fly at two weeks but are not independent until 70–80 days old.

Female is more interested in male's face wattles and the length of the leg spurs than all the other plumage delights.

ABOVE AND BELOW:
FEMALE

FACT FILE

FAMILY Phasianidae (Game Birds). SIZE Length Male 70–90cm. Female 55–70cm. In both cases tail accounts for half of length. FOOD In winter mainly grain and seeds, with other vegetable matter. In summer eats many insects, plus worms and other items. Kills a lot of lizards and snakes. SIMILAR SPECIES Rural areas may hold the Red-legged Partridges (*Alectoris rufa*), which could be confused with a young Pheasant.

| JAN | FEB | MAR | **APR** | **MAY** | **JUN** | **JUL** | **AUG** | SEP | OCT | NOV | DEC |

CUCKOO

Cuculus canorus

Locally common summer visitor, mainly to rural areas and woodland. Declining in the south.

One of the voices of spring, the far-carrying call of this iconic bird can be heard from many rural gardens throughout the region. Catching sight of it is another matter; many people never have. It is very shy and secretive, and has a habit of flying low and silently – if you hear one, try waiting until it has finished a bout of calling, then look for a medium-sized, hawk-like bird with a long tail and pointed wingtips flying rapidly over, the wingbeats remaining below the horizontal. It needs to be furtive. Famously, it subcontracts breeding duties to small, insectivorous songbirds against their will, by laying a single egg in a host's nest and removing one of the host's own. The young Cuckoo hatches early and straightaway pushes the rival eggs or young out of the nest. Common hosts include Dunnock (p. 130), Meadow Pipit (p. 132) and Robin (p. 120), as well as Reed Warbler (*Acrocephalus scirpaceus*).

A Cuckoo is roughly pigeon sized, but with pointed wings and a long tail, so looks like a hawk. However, when flying, it does not raise its wings above horizontal, so looks a bit odd. When perched, it often droops the wings and tail. Note the small, curved bill. **ADULT** Mainly smoky-grey with white underparts barred with black. There are white spots on the tail, and the eye is yellow. **FEMALE** Often has

FACT FILE

FAMILY Cuculidae (Cuckoos). SIZE Length 32–36cm. Wingspan 54–60cm. FOOD Variety of insects, with a particular fondness for hairy caterpillars. SIMILAR SPECIES Pigeons (pp. 20–25), Kestrel (p. 40) and Sparrowhawk (p. 38).

brown on chest. A few individuals are warm brown on the back. **JUVENILE** Similar to adults but barred on head, and has narrow white bars above and a white patch on nape. **VOICE** Famous, sonorous *cuck-oo* audible from a great distance. Varies a lot; sometimes has three syllables. Female utters loud, excited ringing trill, like a Green Woodpecker's (p. 46), but stays on same pitch; also a coughing sound. **MIGRATION** Migrates to forests of Central Africa, stopping off in West African forests en route.

 BREEDING Lays eggs April–June. **NEST** Builds no nest but instead lays an egg in nest of host (see opposite). Foster parents bring up the young Cuckoo alone. **INCUBATION** Growth begins in female's oviduct, so young take only 11–13 days to hatch, faster than host's young. **YOUNG** Stay in nest for about 16 days. Fed outside the nest for 2–3 weeks.

A female Cuckoo lays eggs in the nest of the species that raised it: a female brought up by Meadow Pipits, for example, will seek out Meadow Pipit nests when it comes to breed. If none is available, it may then use other hosts.

Tracking has shown that adult Cuckoos leave northern Europe incredibly early – they may be back in Africa by July.

slim with small head

often droops wings

| JAN | FEB | MAR | APR | MAY | JUN | JUL | AUG | SEP | OCT | NOV | DEC |

FERAL PIGEON

Columba livia

Abundant around human habitation, also cliffs.

This pigeon is a close associate of humankind, found throughout the world in towns, cities and gardens. It has a long history of domestication, for food, racing and sending messages. Birds have been interbred to such an extent that no two individuals look quite alike – so one way to know you are seeing this species is to appreciate the variety in its flocks. The bird is more common in truly urban rather than suburban gardens, where flocks live in parks and built-up areas. They come to grain in town squares and live in public buildings such as stations, and flocks from pigeon lofts often fly overhead in circles. Groups often loaf for hours on favoured roofs. Feral Pigeons are famous for shamelessly displaying in public, ruffling their feathers, fanning the tail and cooing at their chosen fancy.

white cere on top of bill

red eyes

The species is smaller than a Wood Pigeon, with a shorter tail. It has a fast, powerful flapping flight with loud wing-flaps, sounding rather like somebody cutting through bread with a knife very quickly. It is usually whitish under the wing. **ADULT** Occurs in variety packs of many colours and patterns. Pink legs and red eyes. Bill has a white 'cere' above it (like a noseband). **JUVENILE** Barely distinguishable from adult. **VOICE** Song a quiet, crooning *coo* with a slight stammer, rendered as 'Look at the MOOON'. **MIGRATION** Hardly ever moves far at all, but homing pigeons do (see below).

ABOVE: *WHITISH UNDERWINGS IN FLIGHT*

BREEDING Famous for breeding in every month of the year; often produces three broods but in theory could churn out five. **NEST** Placed inside a crevice, usually in a building or other such construction, a feeble pile of twigs, sticks, litter, even wire – whatever is available. Colonial nester. **EGGS** Two, incubated for 17–19 days. **YOUNG** Fed on crop milk (p. 23) and leave nest after three weeks or so; fed until 30–35 days old.

The Pigeon Life Mystery – why do we never seen baby pigeons? The answer is that young pigeons do not leave the nest until they are so similar to the adults that you can't tell the difference.

BELOW: *VARIANT*

Feral Pigeons are the same as homing pigeons, which are famed for their incredible powers of navigation and finding their lofts when flying over vast distances. Yet in the wild, they barely ever leave their neighbourhood.

FACT FILE

FAMILY Columbidae (Pigeons and Doves). **SIZE** Length 30–35cm. Wingspan 62–68cm. **FOOD** Grain, seeds, bread, scraps. **SIMILAR SPECIES** Wood Pigeon (p. 24) and Stock Dove (p. 22); in flight perhaps Collared Dove (p. 26).

| JAN | FEB | MAR | APR | MAY | JUN | JUL | AUG | SEP | OCT | NOV | DEC |

STOCK DOVE

Columba oenas

Fairly common in larger, reasonably well wooded gardens, as well as parks and agricultural areas.

This species is something of a birdwatcher's secret; most people do not even know that the Stock Dove exists, or are even aware that they have seen one. In truth, though, these gentle doves are usually just overlooked, due to their similarity to much more common pigeons. However, they are quite common in rural gardens over much of the region. You tend to see just one or two. They lack the overbearing nature of other pigeons and doves. Their song is gentle, and their displays are subtle, just a circular flight and glide with wings in a 'V'.

The Stock Dove is similar in size to the Feral Pigeon (p. 20), but considerably smaller than the Wood Pigeon (p. 24). It is more squat and compact than either, with a shorter tail, but the differences are far from obvious. **ADULT** The dark eye is a clincher (Feral Pigeon red, Wood Pigeon yellow). No white neck-patch, only an emerald-green one. Gorgeous subtle pink breast. Two short black bars. In flight, underwings pale, upperwings dove-grey centred (may look white). **VOICE** Song a soft *coo* that is as easily missed as the bird itself. It is simply three notes, *oo-oo-oo*, up-down-up, with the sort of disapproving tone an elderly aunt might adopt towards a teenage dress code. **MIGRATION** Resident in Britain, France and the Low Countries; Scandinavian and Baltic birds migrate south in winter.

FACT FILE

FAMILY Columbidae (Pigeons and Doves). SIZE Length 28–32cm. Wingspan 60–66cm. FOOD Seeds, grain, leaves, buds, taken from the ground. SIMILAR SPECIES Feral Pigeon; also Wood Pigeon, which has yellow eyes and white on neck and wings.

BREEDING Breeds April–September, amassing up to four broods, but two are more usual. **NEST** In a hole, usually in a tree, but also cliff, building or even rabbit hole; hardly any nest material used. **EGGS** Two, incubated for 16–18 days by both sexes. **YOUNG** Fed on crop milk, taken direct from adults' open mouth. They leave the nest at 27–28 days after hatching, sometimes less.

Members of the pigeon family are unusual for feeding their young on 'crop milk', a semi-liquid substance made from cells peeling off from the crop walls.

black eyes

small black bar on wing

| JAN | FEB | MAR | APR | MAY | JUN | JUL | AUG | SEP | OCT | NOV | DEC |

WOOD PIGEON

Columba palumbus

Abundant in much of region but scarcer to the north.

You might not love it, but you can hardly miss it. One of the most abundant birds in the region, the Wood Pigeon is everywhere, from city centres to isolated farms and homesteads. Little seems to endear it to people, from its dull familiarity to its predilection for farmers' crops and certain garden plants – it is often chastised for coming to feeders and taking food meant for more 'attractive' birds. Yet it provides great entertainment. Paired couples often sit side by side on roofs or wires and preen each other, apparently enraptured. Males often chase flustered mates, metaphorically stepping on their toes. And all summer long, Wood Pigeons launch into a splendid display-flight, rising upwards on rapid wingbeats, stalling with a loud wing-clap as if shot, then sailing down to another perch, following a line (see Collared

yellow eyes

white neck patch

Dove, p. 26). Delightfully, these birds are utterly incompetent nest builders, with the feeble stick platform so flimsy that you can sometimes see the eggs from below. The Wood Pigeon is a big garden character.

white flashes on wings

The species is bigger and portlier than other pigeons or doves, with a tummy like a beer gut. Remember that all individuals look the same, unlike Feral Pigeons. The birds are fast and powerful, with the tail looking long. **ADULT** Look for yellow eyes, a large and messy white patch on the neck, and a white bar on the wing. At rest, the feathers of the wingtips are edged with white. In flight, the white bands across the middle of the wing are the clincher. **JUVENILE** Unfortunately lacks the white neck-patch. **VOICE** Song is one of the sounds of summer suburbia, not that everyone appreciates it. It is a cooing phrase with five notes, a quick introduction followed by two slow, emphasized notes and two quick notes to finish – 'Take TWO COOS, Colin', or 'Oh DEAR HOW boring'. The cooing has a gorgeous sauciness, of the very gentlest kind. **MIGRATION** Resident in most of the region, but Baltic and Scandinavian birds migrate south within Europe for winter.

BREEDING In theory breeds at any time of year, but there is a peak in summer. **NEST** A cowboy builder's flimsy platform of twigs, in a tree or bush. **EGGS** Two, incubated for 17 days. **YOUNG** Remain in nest for 29–35 days, fed on crop milk (p. 23).

Wood Pigeons eat quite a lot of snails. In one crop from a dead bird, five species were found.

FACT FILE

FAMILY Columbidae (Pigeons and Doves). SIZE Length 38–43cm. Wingspan 68–77cm. FOOD Wide variety of plant material, some guaranteed to make gardeners see red, and also crops to make farmers see red; also clover and many other leaves, seeds and berries (especially of ivy). SIMILAR SPECIES Feral Pigeon (p. 20), and also Stock Dove (p. 22), which has dark eyes and lacks any white on neck or wings.

| JAN | FEB | MAR | APR | MAY | JUN | JUL | AUG | SEP | OCT | NOV | DEC |

COLLARED DOVE

Streptopelia decaocto

Locally common, especially in suburban areas.

You wonder what Collared Doves did before rooftops were invented because this is where they thrive. In many parts of the region, their dirge-like cooing provides an almost continuous soundtrack, one that emanates from aerials and other high spots in any month of the year, especially throughout the long summer. Rooftops also provide a perfect launch-pad for their eye-catching display: they flap hard to rise at a steep angle, often with wing-claps, reach their designated height, then spiral down to a different elevated perch, their wings and tail spread. Suburbia is the Collared Dove's hub; it does not occur in woods or forests, and not always in agricultural areas, but gardens are its dream location. It is even better for them if kind householders provide seed and grain, too. Overall, Collared Doves are less sociable than Feral and Wood Pigeons (pp. 20 and 24), and are usually just seen in pairs.

This is a relatively slim, streamlined dove with a long tail. It flies with a distinctive 'flicking' action of the wings, rather than the consistent,

FACT FILE

FAMILY Columbidae (Pigeons and Doves). FOOD Seeds and grain, some berries and insects. SIZE Length 29–33cm. Wingspan 48–53cm. SIMILAR SPECIES Other pigeons and doves. The Turtle Dove (*S. turtur*) is still found in some gardens, especially in France, but has all but disappeared elsewhere. It has a stunning tortoiseshell pattern on the back and a black-and-white neck-patch.

thin black-and-white neck-ring

white tail tip

overall soft, anaemic colouring

constant flapping of other pigeons and doves. **ADULT** Slightly sickly milky-brown with a black half-collar. Tail has white tips. **JUVENILE** Lacks black neck-collar. **VOICE** Makes a famous three-note cooing dirge that is easily rendered as the chant of a football fan: 'Un-I-ted'. This is one of the sounds of the suburban garden in the summer, heard long after many other birds have fallen silent. Upon alighting, gives an odd nasal call like a party-blower. **MIGRATION** Resident, although young birds may disperse hundreds of kilometres.

BREEDING Can breed at any time of year and produce almost continuously, although mainly March–October. **NEST** Placed in a tree (often a Leylandii), and is a platform of thin twigs that does not look adequate for the task. **EGGS** Two, incubated for 15 days. **YOUNG** Fed by crop milk (p. 23). Can fly at about 18 days.

 Singing a three-note *coo* is apparently too much for some males. They only do two, much to the disgust of potential mates.

 Not surprisingly, Collared Doves can sometimes complete building a nest in a day.

| JAN | FEB | MAR | APR | MAY | JUN | JUL | AUG | SEP | OCT | NOV | DEC |

BLACK-HEADED GULL

Chroicocephalus ridibundus

Generally abundant near freshwater, coastal areas.

When is a seagull not a sea gull? When it's a Black-headed Gull. Some people still seem to think that when gulls come inland it is a freak event, perhaps caused by a storm at sea. But this is just not true. Many Black-headed Gulls spend all winter inland, never seeing the sea, but instead spend their time commuting between fields – where they forage in flocks for worms and other invertebrates – and lakes, where they loaf and roost. They are often abundant on sports grounds and by rivers, and at ponds they compete with ducks for bread. In many places, you can see morning and evening flights of gulls flying over the garden in 'V' formation – these will mostly be Black-headed Gulls. This is a noisy, successful and ubiquitous bird.

RIGHT: *ADULT SUMMER*

BELOW: *ADULT WINTER*

smart, chocolate-brown hood

white eye-ring

The smallest gull of the garden, this species has narrow wings with sharp wingtips and a long, slender bill. The wings always have a conspicuous white (isosceles) triangle from the bend to the tip. **ADULT SUMMER** Chocolate-brown half-hood and half a white eye-ring. **ADULT WINTER** Black smudge behind eye and one coming up from eye. Legs are red. **YOUNG STAGES** Brown on wings and an orange bill. Aging gulls are a bottomless pit as far as identification is concerned. **VOICE** Grating *krreaerr*, given with variation and a lot of enthusiasm. **MIGRATION** Scandinavian and Baltic birds migrate south in winter, often only to Britain and the near Continent, where the bird is around all year.

ABOVE LEFT: *ADULT WINTER*

ABOVE: *IMMATURE (1ST WINTER)*

BREEDING April–July, not in gardens, one brood. **NEST** Nests in colonies that create a marvellous ear-splitting din, a few metres apart. Nests are limp aggregations of local vegetation, usually on islands in lakes or wetlands. **EGGS** Usually three, incubated for 23–26 days by both sexes. **YOUNG** Hatch fluffy and mobile, but do not wander far and are fed for about a month.

In mid-summer, Black-headed Gulls often appear in excited groups flying over gardens. This is a sign that it is Flying Ant Day, with the gulls cashing in on the millions of amorous insects on mating flights.

FACT FILE

FAMILY Laridae (Gulls and Terns). SIZE Length: 35–39cm. Wingspan 86–99cm. FOOD Omnivorous – fish, worms, bread, insects. SIMILAR SPECIES Other gulls, but the Herring Gull (p. 32) is much larger.

COMMON GULL

Larus canus

Locally common, especially to north and east. Common inland.

It is never great for the image if you are medium, but medium is exactly what the Common Gull is. It is larger and chunkier than the abundant Black-headed Gull (p. 28), but much smaller than the similarly plumaged Herring Gull (p. 32) – in other words, middle sized with in-between plumage, and that is a classic recipe for being overlooked. It is nonetheless a handsome gull, with a rather beautiful, heavy-cloud-grey mantle and dark, dewdrop eyes. The English name is half a misnomer – it is not the most common gull, but it is numerous throughout the region in winter, and common all year in Scotland and Scandinavia, including inland on lakes and agricultural fields.

This species is just slightly larger than the Black-headed Gull and much less slender, with fulsome, not so obviously pointed wings. The wings have large white blobs at the ends of the black tips. **ADULT SUMMER** A bit of a stunner, with a beautiful white head and dark eye, together with bright yellow legs and yellow bill. **ADULT WINTER** Head becomes frosty with flecks and legs can be anything between grey and green, with the same colour on the bill. **IMMATURE STAGES** Younger birds less than two years old have various confusing plumages, best ignored. **VOICE** Call is an ear-splitting squeal, like a soprano normal gull. **MIGRATION** Migrates south in winter, but usually within Europe; mainly a winter visitor in southern Britain, France and Low Countries.

ADULT WINTER

FACT FILE

FAMILY Laridae (Gulls and Terns). SIZE Length: 35–39cm. Wingspan 86–99cm. FOOD Fish, invertebrates (including worms), small mammals, carrion, berries. SIMILAR SPECIES Other gulls, but the Herring Gull is much larger.

brown flecks on head (adult winter)

dark eye

greenish bill

 BREEDING May–July. **NEST** Nests in colonies, usually on islands in lakes, occasionally on buildings, the nest being an undistinguished pile of vegetation. **EGGS** Three, incubated for 22–27 days by both sexes. **YOUNG** Hatch fluffy and able to run about, and fed for about 35 days.

ABOVE: ADULT WINTER

⭐ Very unusual among gulls in sometimes nesting on tree stumps and branches.

BELOW: IMMATURE (1ST WINTER)

| JAN | FEB | MAR | APR | MAY | JUN | JUL | AUG | SEP | OCT | NOV | DEC |

HERRING GULL

Larus argentatus

Often abundant, mostly in coastal areas; some cities.

This is not just a bird – it is an atmosphere, a definition of place. Nobody who lives by the seaside will be in any doubt about the Herring Gull's omnipotence where humanity meets the sea. This bird is the wailing voice of the rooftops, the beach scavenger and the chip stealer – and the seaside experience is all the better for it. It is the maritime gull, not seen inland so often. It is a large bird, brash and confident, and its yellow eye gives it an angry expression that is intimidating up close. Adaptable, it will eat almost anything, even the leftovers from fast-food outlets, beyond the pale to most other forms of life. This bird is expert at walking, swimming and flying.

The species is large and bulky. If you see the birds in a flock, it is obvious that they occur in a bewildering array of patterns, from streaky-

RIGHT: *IMMATURE (3RD WINTER)*

BELOW: *IMMATURES (1ST WINTER)*

yellow eye

brown to pale grey; this is a matter of age, and the youngest birds are the brownest. It always has pink legs. **ADULT SUMMER** Mean-looking gull that clearly does not have your interests at heart, with a frowning expression and yellow eye. Quite a pale, silvery-grey back. Bill yellow with an orange spot. Insubstantial white spots on wingtips. **ADULT WINTER** Dark flecks on head. **IMMATURE STAGES** Do not go there, dear reader, if you value your sanity. **VOICE** Never quiet and makes a series of wailing and gruff calls. The best known is the 'long call', a series of loud, wailing cries like an early morning bell, only much worse. These have a territorial function. **MIGRATION** Wanders after breeding, with many northern birds retreating south within the region.

ABOVE, LEFT & RIGHT:
ADULT SUMMER

BREEDING April–July, one brood. **NEST** May be on the roof of a house (by the sea or inland) but usually part of a colony on a cliff, sand-dune or island. A substantial pile of vegetation and debris. **EGGS** 2–3, incubated for a month. **YOUNG** Hatch well developed and able to run about, but stay in the territory for another month or so.

Nestling Herring Gulls have been known to sack their parents. If they do not deem the provision of food as adequate, they take their lives in their hands and move next door.

Herring Gulls quite often form female-female pairs. One mates and produces eggs, but the young are raised in a feminine household.

FACT FILE

FAMILY Laridae (Gulls and Terns). SIZE Length: 54–60cm. Wingspan 123–148cm. FOOD Omnivore, eating fish, carrion and scraps. Some individuals enjoy chips. Steals from other birds as well as holidaymakers. SIMILAR SPECIES Other gulls. Much larger than the Black-headed Gull (p. 28).

JAN	FEB	MAR	APR	MAY	JUN	JUL	AUG	SEP	OCT	NOV	DEC

BUZZARD

Buteo buteo

Common and widespread, mainly open country with woods.

Over most of the region, this is the largest bird of prey that you are likely to see over a garden. It tends to avoid built-up areas, but in the countryside, you see it everywhere – if you drive in the country, you are likely to see it perched on poles or fences. It does not use gardens, but look up and you might see a chunky bird of prey with very broad wings, a rounded head and a noticeably short tail. It is remarkably adaptable in its foraging, one moment diving down on a young rabbit, the next moment waddling over mud hoping to pick up worms (especially in the rain). It can soar, it can hover and it can drop down from a low perch to snap up something edible. In the spring, listen out for its gorgeous, atmospheric calls.

This is easily the biggest bird of prey seen from a garden, dwarfing crows, for example. It has broad wings, a short tail (the same length as the wings are broad) that is often fanned, and a small, broad head. It flies straight ahead with quick, stiff wingbeats followed by a short glide. When soaring, it lifts its wings in a shallow 'V'. It sometimes hovers.

ADULT Extremely variable. Most birds are dark brown, but some look almost white. Adults usually have neat, dark tail-band at tip. **JUVENILE** No dark tail-band. **VOICE** Gives a wild-sounding *mew*, with a definite complaining air. **MIGRATION** Mainly resident.

BREEDING April–June, one brood. **NEST** Bulky platform of sticks and other materials, often reused, in branches of a tree or on a rocky outcrop. **EGGS** 3–4, but varies a lot, incubated for 33–35 days.

FACT FILE

FAMILY Accipitridae (Diurnal Birds of Prey). SIZE Length 48–56cm. Wingspan 113–128cm.
FOOD Hunter of small mammals and birds; also takes roadkill, plus worms and insects.
SIMILAR SPECIES Red Kite (p. 36). There is a variety of raptors in Britain and other parts of
Europe of vaguely similar shape, but few occur in gardens.

YOUNG Downy, and leave nest at about 50 days; they make continuous loud, pleading whistles to parents.

⭐ Look out for the display, in which the male flies up, closes its wings, and dives down until just before it hits the treetops, before looping up again. It sometimes dives down as much as 60m, which must be fun.

rounded head →

RED KITE

Milvus milvus

Fairly common but localized, open country; most common population in UK recently reintroduced.

In recent years this magnificent bird has become a regular sight over British gardens, although it is much rarer on the Continent. Some people treat their local Red Kites with thrown-out meat and other scraps, which makes a change from feeding sparrows or pigeons, so who can blame them? The Red Kite essentially earns its living by being a scavenger, seeking out dead meat such as roadkill. This is one of the masters of the air, able to move with grace with no more than a flick of the wings or a twitch of that magnificent forked tail.

It is a large bird of prey, as big as a Buzzard (p. 34), but slimmer with that ultra-distinctive long, forked tail. If you see it from a distance, note that it holds its wings horizontally or even slightly arced downwards, whether it is gliding or soaring. **ADULT** Body and tail a beautiful reddish colour, head almost bluish-white. **VOICE** Call is like that of a Buzzard with a long tail – yes, really. It is a *mew* followed by a series of short *mew*s – a cat followed by several kittens. **MIGRATION** Mainly resident.

glorious reddish plumage

bluish head

BREEDING March–June, one brood. **NEST** Large platform of sticks and debris, such as human rubbish, often placed on top of an old Buzzard nest, in a tree. **EGGS** 1–3, incubated for 28–30 days, during which the male brings food to the female. **YOUNG** Hatch covered in down and leave nest at about 40 days old, but remain dependent for a month or so.

Kites used to attend the gallows and battlegrounds in many parts of Europe. The English sixteenth/ seventeenth-century playwright William Shakespeare made several less than flattering remarks about them.

FACT FILE

FAMILY Accipitridae (Diurnal Birds of Prey). SIZE Length 61–72cm. Wingspan 175–195cm. FOOD Specializes on dead meat (carrion), often roadkill, but very capable of catching small mammals, birds and insects. SIMILAR SPECIES Buzzard. The Black Kite (*Milvus migrans*), found in northern France and Germany, is similar but with a shallower tail-fork and less reddish colour.

| JAN | FEB | MAR | APR | MAY | JUN | JUL | AUG | SEP | OCT | NOV | DEC |

SPARROWHAWK

Accipiter nisus

Common but secretive.

This is the most familiar garden raider of birdfeeders. You often see the reaction of other birds before you see the Sparrowhawk itself, as the chirpy atmosphere of the feeding station is shattered by a suddenly deathly silence and all hands fleeing. Have no fear, though – Sparrowhawks take an inevitable toll of garden birds, but the presence of these raptors is a sign of a decent bird population. This is a secretive hunter, which spends much time concealed until its sudden bursts in level flight towards bird flocks. However, it does often soar above gardens, progressing upwards with rapid flaps followed by glides, often mobbed by smaller birds. Once it has caught prey it usually carries it away, but may stay to pluck and eat its food, which makes for a gruesome garden drama.

This is a small raptor, only pigeon sized, but muscular and powerful. In the garden, it is usually seen ambushing birds or possibly perching

very upright on a fence or tree, when you can see the yellow legs and feet. The yellow eyes confer a maniacally fierce expression. The breast is distinctively barred. It flies and soars in a distinctive way, employing glides interspersed with a burst of quick flaps. Long tail, blunt-ended wings. **MALE** Small, with orange wash to breast and bluish upperparts. **FEMALE** Larger, with pale breast and greyish upperparts. **JUVENILE** Confusing, with brown upperparts and disrupted bars on the breast. **VOICE** A series of rapid *kek* calls, sounding irritated. **MIGRATION** Mainly resident, but some northern and eastern populations move south in autumn.

FACT FILE

FAMILY Accipitridae (Diurnal Birds of Prey). SIZE Length: Male 29–34cm. Female 35–41cm. Wingspan: male 59–65cm. Female 68–77cm. FOOD Almost entirely birds, caught by ambush. Similar species: Kestrel (p. 40). Very similar, but larger and bulkier Goshawk (*Accipiter gentilis*) may visit continental gardens, although it is rare in Britain.

BREEDING April–July, one brood. **NEST** Placed in a tree, in a fork or near the trunk; well hidden. It is a platform of sticks. **EGGS** 4–5, incubated by female, and fed for 35–40 days. **YOUNG** Downy young remain in nest for about a month, fed for the first 4–5 days by the male only, and later by both parents.

Males eat small birds such as tits and finches, while females, which are bigger, take larger birds like doves and Starlings (p. 102). It helps to prevent competition between the sexes.

ABOVE: *MALE*

LEFT: *JUVENILE*

staring yellow eyes

broken bars on breast

JAN	FEB	MAR	APR	MAY	JUN	JUL	AUG	SEP	OCT	NOV	DEC

KESTREL

Falco tinnunculus

Fairly common in open areas, including farmland.

If ever a bird was closely associated with its feeding method, it would be the Kestrel, an inveterate hoverer. It is not a particularly familiar garden bird, but it is often a neighbourhood bird, drawn to small patches of rough grassland where there is a healthy population of its favourite food, small mammals. It often perches on overhead wires and pounces down on food from a height. More often it hovers, wings beating rapidly, tail spread and head perfectly still, constantly adjusting its body with the vagaries of the breeze, but keeping its gazed fixed on the long grass below.

This is a relatively small raptor with a noticeably long tail, and always shows at least some rusty plumage. It is slimmer than a Sparrowhawk (p. 38), but has a much looser, flappier flight. Crucially, a Kestrel's wings usually look decidedly pointed, while those of a Sparrowhawk are more blunt ended. The long tail is rounded at the tip, not square. In flight, the outer wings are dark and the inner wings rusty. **MALE** A very handsome bird, with a grey head and grey tail with one large black band just before tip. **FEMALE** Barred rusty-brown, with streaks down breast and multiple extra bands on tail. **VOICE** Hoarse, ringing call, not often heard. **MIGRATION** Mainly resident, but populations in north and east of the region may be long-distance migrants to Africa.

BELOW: *FEMALE*

brown head

heavily barred back

LEFT: *MALE HAS GREY HEAD, GREY TAIL AND ONE BROAD BLACK TERMINAL BAND*

BELOW: *FEMALE, HOVERING, HAS MANY BANDS ON TAIL*

 BREEDING March–June, one brood. **NEST** Does not build one. Instead simply lays eggs on a ledge (on a cliff or tall building) or in a treehole. **EGGS** 4-5, incubated by female for 28-29 days; fed by male. **YOUNG** Remain in nest for about 35 days, and for the first 12-20 days are fed only by the hard-working male.

★ Young Kestrels leave the nest and may then disperse up to 150km.

FACT FILE

FAMILY Falconidae (Falcons). SIZE Length 31–37cm. Wingspan 65–82cm. FOOD Mainly small mammals such as voles, but also eats small birds and insects, especially large beetles. SIMILAR SPECIES Sparrowhawk.

| JAN | FEB | MAR | APR | MAY | JUN | JUL | AUG | SEP | OCT | NOV | DEC |

LONG-EARED OWL

Asio otus

Locally fairly common but very secretive.

This gorgeous owl is more widespread in the region than the more common Tawny Owl (p. 44), occurring in Ireland and over much more of Norway and Sweden, but it is a mysterious and poorly known neighbour. It can sometimes be seen in parks or large gardens in winter, where it gathers in small groups, but is very secretive when breeding. In common with the Tawny Owl it is largely nocturnal, but its hunting method is completely different; instead of hunting from a perch, it flies low and stealthily over open ground, diving down when it detects food, usually a small mammal. It can hunt in complete darkness, suggesting that it can detect prey using hearing alone. However, the famous 'ears' that make it so distinctive are not ears at all, merely tufts of feathers at the ear openings. The tufts break up the

long wings for buoyant flight

pale orange eyes

FACT FILE

FAMILY Strigidae (Owls). SIZE Length 31–37cm. Wingspan 86–98cm. FOOD Mainly small mammals, especially voles; a few birds. SIMILAR SPECIES Tawny Owl.

owl's head silhouette, perhaps helping it to avoid detection by larger predators. At any rate, the ear-tufts can betray emotion, being raised when the owl is alarmed or excited.

This is a big, upright, long-winged owl (still smaller than the Tawny Owl). Its flight style is very different from a Tawny Owl's, freer and more wavering. At rest the ear-tufts are usually obvious. **ADULT** Facial expression unmistakable, with the orange eyes and whitish 'V' between them. **VOICE** Hoot is a slow series of notes like a distant foghorn. Young have a call just like a squeaky gate. **MIGRATION** Many resident, but birds from east and north are migratory and will cross the North Sea in autumn and spring. More move in years with fewer voles available.

BREEDING February–June, one brood. **NEST** Does not build its own nest, but instead commandeers an old nest of a Magpie (p. 56) or other crow, or the drey of a squirrel. **EGGS** 4–5, sometimes more when there is lots of prey about. Incubation lasts 25–30 days, beginning with the first, which leads to large age differences among the young. **YOUNG** Leave nest after a month, fed by male alone for most of that time.

Although a hunter itself, the Long-eared Owl is often caught and eaten by other raptors, especially Goshawks (*Accipiter gentilis*) – more than any other European owl.

TAWNY OWL

Strix aluco

Common, even in towns and cities, but nocturnal.

In most of Britain and continental Europe this is the most common owl in gardens, the main one responsible for the gorgeous, atmospheric hooting that can be heard from autumn, right through winter and into spring. This owl is highly adaptable and occurs deep in the heart of major cities, where it feeds on rats, mice and birds, as well as in suburban and rural gardens. It is highly nocturnal, but quite happy to use the light from street lamps for hunting, sometimes perching on the lamps themselves and flying down to pounce on prey. Lawns are also ideal, since they provide short grass with little chance of concealment for prey. Tawny Owls are very faithful to their territories

and remain in the same place for life, sometimes longer than their human neighbours.

This big owl with a very round head tends to perch upright. In common with all owls it flies silently, but unlike the Long-eared Owl (p. 42) it has stiff wingbeats, which it alternates with glides. **ADULT** Usually a rich stew of different browns, with streaks, spots and stripes. Some individuals are greyer, without the typical warm tone. **VOICE** Most hooting is done by males. When advertising their territory, they make an introductory hoot, pause for a few seconds, then make a spine-tingling, quavering hoot sequence, one that everyone has heard on film soundtracks. Both sexes also utter a sharp *ke-wick* that acts as a contact call. **MIGRATION** Resident.

rounded head

black eyes

BREEDING February–May. **NEST** Does not make a nest, but lays eggs straight into hole in tree, rock crevice or nest-box. **EGGS** 2–4, incubated by female only for 28–30 days. **YOUNG** Fed on meat by male for first three weeks, then both sexes hunt. Owlets leave nest at 32–37 days but are dependent for another three months.

A Tawny Owl sees better than a human in the dark, but only by a factor of 1.8.

FACT FILE

FAMILY Strigidae (Owls). SIZE Length 37–43cm. Wingspan 81–96cm. FOOD Small mammals and birds, plus insects, frogs and worms. SIMILAR SPECIES Long-eared Owl. In rural areas look out for the Barn Owl (*Tyto alba*), of similar size but with overall pale plumage, ghostly white below. It has a heart-shaped face and black eyes.

JAN	FEB	MAR	APR	MAY	JUN	JUL	AUG	SEP	OCT	NOV	DEC

GREEN WOODPECKER

Picus viridis

Locally common in parks and woodland edges.

A bird you are far more likely to see on your lawn than in a tree, the Green Woodpecker is unusual among garden birds for having just one very dominant food source – ants. So it eschews the usual woodpecker lifestyle of pecking at dead wood, and instead pecks into anthills on the ground, where it may remain for many minutes just lapping up the workers as they try to protect the soil-based colony. It has a long tongue that protrudes 10cm beyond the bill-tip, and coated with sticky saliva, it is perfect for lapping up ants from cracks in trees

BELOW: *MALE*

red crown

red moustache

green colouration

FACT FILE

FAMILY Picidae (Woodpeckers). SIZE Length 31–33cm. Wingspan 45–51cm. FOOD Almost entirely ants, even in winter. SIMILAR SPECIES Other woodpeckers. On the Continent the very similar Grey-headed Woodpecker (*Picus canus*) occurs in larger gardens. It has a grey head with only a very thin black moustache, and is more of a conventional woodpecker, living in the trees.

and other surfaces. When disturbed, the Green Woodpecker makes a loud, laughing call, often the first indicator of its presence, and flies with a heavily undulating, up-and-down flight to the nearest tree trunk. It continues to eat ants in winter, even digging under snow to find them.

Once you realize it is a woodpecker it is unmistakable. It is big, larger than a pigeon, with subtle green colouration, a staring white eye and a crimson crown. In flight it gives bursts of flaps, usually not flying very high. **MALE** Not only has a red crown, but also a red centre to its black moustache. The female just has a black streak. **VOICE** A yelping, laughing, slightly overloud and panicky call, as if suddenly worrying the joke it had just made was inappropriate. **MIGRATION** Resident.

ABOVE: *JUVENILE*

BELOW: *FEMALE (BLACK MOUSTACHE)*

BREEDING March–June, one brood. **NEST** A hole it makes itself in a mature tree, with no nesting material. Entrance is about 7cm in diameter. **EGGS** 5–7, incubated for 18–19 days by both sexes. **YOUNG** Fed on regurgitated liquefied ant mush – it must be a treat. They leave at 23–27 days.

★ You can identify the poo of a Green Woodpecker on your lawn: it looks like a disposed cylinder of cigarette ash, with ant exoskeleton fragments in the middle.

★ A single family with seven chicks are thought to have consumed 1.5 million ants during a single breeding attempt.

★ Green Woodpeckers have been known to roost on the ground in rabbit holes!

| JAN | FEB | MAR | APR | MAY | JUN | JUL | AUG | SEP | OCT | NOV | DEC |

GREAT SPOTTED WOODPECKER

Dendrocopos major

Widespread and common; the woodpecker most often seen.

This is by far the most common woodpecker in gardens, and you need to take a very careful look if you think you have another species. It is a bold, adaptable bird that regularly comes to hanging garden feeders, typically making every other rival flee when it makes an appearance – few birds are a match for it. Its main life is lived up in the trees, where it spends much of its time holding on to vertical tree trunks, using its two feet and stiffened tail as a three-sided pivot. The chisel-shaped bill is used to excavate holes in wood, usually dead wood, where a steady supply of invertebrates is found year round. It has a specially stiffened skull to absorb the shock of hole making. It also has a long tongue that seeks out invertebrates hidden in nooks and crannies, and even on leaves. The powerful bill is perfect for opening nuts and seeds, its main winter diet.

The species is about the size of a thrush or Starling (p. 102), but its bold black-and-white plumage makes it look bigger. It is usually seen clinging vertically. The large head, powerful, dagger-shaped bill and short tail are distinctive. **ADULT** Both sexes have a large white 'blob of paint' on the shoulder and an unmarked black back, and both have a crimson patch under the tail. **MALE** Has a red patch on the nape (the female does not). **JUVENILES** Red cap, bigger in male than female.

red nape (male)

white blob on shoulder

red under-tail

ABOVE RIGHT: *JUVENILE*

All woodpeckers have a distinctive flight, using intermittent bursts of the wings to travel a strongly undulating path. **VOICE** 'Song' is the drumming sound make by beating wood rapidly with the bill. This is a seasonal, territorial sound and the birds (both male and female) select wood with sonorous properties to produce the far-carrying message. It is heard from January into spring. It is fast and short, with an attack at the beginning and a sharp fade. Call is a distinctive, loud *chip* or *tchik* – as if chipping wood. Once you recognize it, you will hear it a lot. **MIGRATION** Mainly resident.

BREEDING April–June. **NEST** Bores holes (5–6cm diameter) in trees, usually dead ones, all year round and uses one about 30cm deep for nest. **EGGS** 4–6, incubated for 15 days. **YOUNG** Leave nest at 20 days; often call noisily from the nest-hole long before that.

It sometimes feeds its young on a niche diet – the nestlings of small birds, especially tits. It easily bores into the nest-boxes or holes used by these species.

FACT FILE

FAMILY Picidae (Woodpeckers). **SIZE** Length 23–26cm. Wingspan 38–44cm. **FOOD** Various insects, especially wood-boring beetles, as well as seeds and nuts in winter. **SIMILAR SPECIES** Lesser Spotted Woodpecker (p. 48). There are other similar woodpecker species on the Continent, including the Middle Spotted Woodpecker (*Dendrocopos medius*), which might visit large gardens with old trees. It has streaks down the breast and both sexes have a complete crimson crown.

LESSER SPOTTED WOODPECKER

Dryobates minor

Fairly common to rare; always secretive and elusive.

MALE

Many people think they have Lesser Spotted Woodpeckers in their gardens, but do not realize how much smaller they are than Great Spotted Woodpeckers (p. 48) – not much bigger than a sparrow or Nuthatch (p. 98). In the UK, these birds are also now very rare, although gardens are still part of their habitat, while they are still doing all right in Scandinavia. But a garden visit is always a special event, and a visit to a feeder quite exceptional. This dapper woodpecker

crimson crown

small bill

white stripes like rungs of ladder on back

FACT FILE

FAMILY Picidae (Woodpeckers). SIZE Length 14–16.5cm. Wingspan 24–29cm. FOOD Insects, including wood-boring beetles. SIMILAR SPECIES Great Spotted Woodpecker. Of similar size is another woodpecker, the peculiar Wryneck (*Jynx torquilla*), which is quite common on the Continent. Its ringing call is similar, too, although it is brown and cryptic.

makes quicker, jerkier and more petite movements than the Great Spotted, and is much more restless. It tends to prefer areas with plenty of dead wood, weak-barked trees such as birch and alder, and also tall deciduous trees. It spends large amounts of time high up among thin branches, where it is maddeningly quiet and hard to find.

Expect to be astonished at how small it is. It essentially looks like a much smaller Great Spotted, but the bill is far shorter and thinner. **ADULT** Should be easy to recognize, because it lacks any crimson under the tail, and there are white bars across its back. **MALE** Has a red crown, while female's is black (forehead white). The series of drumming beats is longer and steadier, lacking the attack and quick fade of the Great Spotted Woodpecker's. **VOICE** Listen for the male's distinctive loud, excited peeping call, *pee-pee-pee-pee...*, like an overexuberant alarm clock. The 'chick' call is hardly distinguishable from the Great Spotted's. **MIGRATION** Resident.

FEMALE

 BREEDING April–June, one brood. **NEST** A hole (3–4cm diameter) excavated in a narrow-trunked tree such as birch or alder, with no lining except chippings. **EGGS** 4–8, incubated for 14–15 days. **YOUNG** Leave nest at 18–20 days.

 It sometimes turns up in hedgerows and even reed beds, and joins roaming mixed flocks of birds.

 Ten per cent of all female Lesser Spotted Woodpeckers have two mates, and they are 40 per cent more successful in fledging young than monogamous females.

| JAN | FEB | MAR | APR | MAY | JUN | JUL | AUG | SEP | OCT | NOV | DEC |

RING-NECKED PARAKEET

Psittacula krameri

Very localized, mostly in cities, where can be common.

Parakeets have been found in parts of the UK, France, the Low Countries and Germany since the 1960s, but many people are still surprised to see such 'tropical' birds on the loose in our towns and cities. This species is found naturally in the Sahel region of both Africa and India, so its ability to survive our winters, having been introduced, is pretty impressive. The key is food, and it is greatly helped by gardeners who leave out food, probably mostly intended for other species. Once parakeets land at a feeder, however, other birds flee, unable to hold their ground against the parakeets' formidable bills. For this reason, parakeets are not always popular with householders, and the relationship can be further strained by this bird's incessant piercing

FEMALE (LEFT); MALE (RIGHT)

rose and black neck ring

screeching, which is exotic and intriguing at first, but can grate when the birds become regular. Parakeets are sociable, often roosting in large numbers and foraging in small parties.

This is a streamlined bird with a long tail and sharply pointed wings. Once seen, it is very obvious, with the apple-green plumage and contrasting red bill. **MALE** Difficult to see, thin black ring around head and nape, bordered by gorgeous ring of rose-pink (it is sometimes called the Rose-ringed Parakeet). **FEMALE** Just faint rings around neck. **JUVENILE** As female, but shorter tail. **VOICE** Shrill, piercing shriek, often delivered in loud volleys, followed by other volleys and on and on. If you have parakeets, the call will be seared into your memory! **MIGRATION** Resident.

ABOVE: *MALE*

 BREEDING Remarkably, often starts nesting in January, presumably a throwback to its wild state in India or Africa, but it may still be going in mid-summer. **NEST** Does not exist as such; there is just a nest-site in a hole in a tree. Female lays eggs directly on to floor in hole. **EGGS** Four, incubated for 22–24 days by female, fed by male. **YOUNG** Leave nest at eight weeks.

 Europe is the only continent other than Antarctica with no native parrots, so we have sorted that now.

In Asia, the parakeet is regarded as a pest, taking maize, millet, groundnuts, sorghum, cultivated fruits and guava, among other foods.

FACT FILE

FAMILY Psittacidae (Parrots). SIZE Length 37–43cm. Wingspan 42–48cm. FOOD Wide vegetarian menu: seeds, flowers, leaves, nuts and so on. SIMILAR SPECIES None native, but note that there are quite a few feral parakeet species flying around European towns and cities.

| JAN | FEB | MAR | APR | MAY | JUN | JUL | AUG | SEP | OCT | NOV | DEC |

JAY

Garrulus glandarius

Common but shy, chiefly wooded areas.

It is impossible not to be excited by the sight of a Jay in the garden. Not only are these birds clad in unusual bold colours, with their pink bodies and kingfisher-blue wing-coverts, but they also have an unmistakable wild and shy manner that adds to their charisma, making a garden visit feel like a state visit. In the garden they occasionally visit tray-type feeders, especially early in the morning, but are more likely to hop on the lawn, looking for invertebrates or, in season, nuts. Jays have a remarkable relationship with oak trees, spending much of the autumn seeking out acorns and storing them in their territory. This activity makes them suddenly obvious, since finding acorns might require commuting movements over some distances. Jays are also inveterate robbers of the nests of small birds, and undoubtedly cause more damage than Magpies (p. 56).

This is an unmistakable colourful crow. It makes confident hops on the ground. The flight is somewhat unsteady-looking and fluttery. **ADULT** Note that it has a black tail and white rump, easy to see as it

FACT FILE

FAMILY Corvidae (Crows). SIZE Length 32–35cm. Wingspan 50cm. FOOD Omnivorous, eating everything from nuts and seeds (especially acorns) to small birds, their eggs and young. SIMILAR SPECIES None, but the Magpie has a similar flight action.

pink plumage

kingfisher-blue wing-patch

flies off. **JUVENILE** Not much different from adult. **CALL** You cannot miss this harsh, swearing screech with an uncomfortable angry, tearing vibe. The name 'Jay' comes from the call. It is one of the ugliest garden bird sounds. **MIGRATION** Mainly resident, but on the Continent thousands may move in the autumn if there are not many acorns about.

BREEDING April–June, one brood. **NEST** Carefully hidden away in a tree, often at a fork. It is a cup of sticks and roots, with some earth, lined with finer materials. **EGGS** 5–7, incubated by female for 16–17 days. **YOUNG** Leave nest at three weeks.

The Jay is arguably a far more destructive nest predator of small birds than its more famous relative, the Magpie. It just performs it all under cover of vegetation, whereas the Magpie is often caught red-handed.

MAGPIE

Pica pica

Often abundant and easy to see; suburbia suits it. Also hardy.

All the best characters have an edge to them, and the ubiquitous Magpie certainly divides opinion. Handsome, distinctive, noisy and hard to ignore, it will at least not cause any identification headaches. It has a reputation for attacking the nests of small garden birds in spring, and although this undoubtedly happens, it is only a niche activity for a bird that spends most of its time looking for invertebrates on the ground. It also takes carrion from roadkill. Magpies are intelligent and curious birds, highly adaptable and able to thrive in a suburban environment. They have an interesting social life, with some birds living as pairs in a territory, while others remain in flocks all year round. In the evening, though, Magpies often gather together to roost in thick shrubs or trees.

The Magpie is unmistakable, with its stout body and long tail. The tail is longest in the middle ('graduated'). For such a successful bird it seems to be a poor flyer, with a weak, unsteady-looking action.

unique black-and-white body and long tail

ADULT Black with white belly. The black plumage is iridescent in the sun. **JUVENILE** Shorter tail than in adults. **CALL** Very familiar, mischievous chuckle, a call in line with many people's impression of the bird. **MIGRATION** Resident.

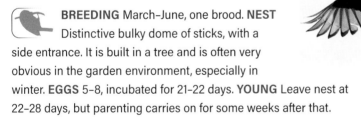

 BREEDING March–June, one brood. **NEST** Distinctive bulky dome of sticks, with a side entrance. It is built in a tree and is often very obvious in the garden environment, especially in winter. **EGGS** 5–8, incubated for 21–22 days. **YOUNG** Leave nest at 22–28 days, but parenting carries on for some weeks after that.

 The length of a Magpie's tail is an indication of its social status. Those with longer tails are dominant.

Remarkably, despite its reputation, it does not steal shiny objects.

 Magpies have a sense of self; in experiments, it has been shown that they recognize their own reflection in a mirror.

FACT FILE

FAMILY Corvidae (Crows). SIZE Length 40–51cm (tail 20–30cm of this). Wingspan 56–61cm. FOOD Omnivorous, but mainly invertebrates in summer and plant material, such as berries, in winter. Also carrion from roadkill. SIMILAR SPECIES None.

| JAN | FEB | MAR | APR | MAY | JUN | JUL | AUG | SEP | OCT | NOV | DEC |

JACKDAW

Corvus monedula

Locally common in some towns, farming areas and coastlands.

The cheerful, sharp *check* call of this diminutive member of the crow family is a common sound in many built-up areas, especially those with chimneys or tall trees, where the birds can find holes for their nests. They are put off by dense urban areas, but suburbs and villages often host colonies. By far the smallest of the black-coloured crows, the Jackdaw lacks some of the more insalubrious habits of crows, such as feasting on roadkill, or even

pale eyes

grey back of head

short bill

FACT FILE

FAMILY Corvidae (Crows). SIZE Length 30–34cm. Wingspan 70–75cm. FOOD Omnivorous, taking a range of grassland invertebrates; also caterpillars and vegetable matter in winter. SIMILAR SPECIES Rook, Carrion Crow (p. 62). Flies in pigeon-like manner.

killing small mammals and birds. Much of the time it simply forages on grassland. It is exceptionally sociable, living in loose colonies, feeding in flocks and, in particular, roosting in large groups in winter. Jackdaws often fill the evening air above woods, forming dense flocks that perform aerobatics in the sky with great playfulness, their piercing calls as sharp as the cold. They are intelligent and curious, and sometimes steal shiny objects (which Magpies do not).

A crow the size of a pigeon, the Jackdaw's smaller size is obvious when it gathers with Rooks (p. 64), which it does often. It has a jaunty strut when it walks. It has a much shorter bill than other black crows, obvious even in flight. Note the fast wingbeats, recalling the pace of a pigeon ('Flap-Jack, as opposed to Slow Crow'). **ADULT** The small bill, white, staring eye and unmistakable grey wash to the head should be obvious. **JUVENILE** Lacks most of the distinctive features above – it must hate birdwatchers. Can be recognized by size and shape. **VOICE** The incessant, sharp *check* or *kya* call is easy to recognize. **MIGRATION** Mainly resident.

 BREEDING April–May, one brood. **NEST** Stick structure placed in a tree-hole, a rocky crevice or a hole in a building, often a chimney. **EGGS** 4–5, incubated for 18–20 days. **YOUNG** Leave nest 28–32 days after hatching.

★ Jackdaws are very faithful to their partners and have an exceptionally low rate of extra-pair paternity (1 per cent).

★ When nesting in chimneys Jackdaws throw down sticks until they lodge, making a platform by trial and error – and a mess!

HOODED CROW

Corvus cornix

Locally common in any habitat. Very hardy.

This is the tough northern and eastern version of the Carrion Crow (p. 62), replacing it in Scandinavia, Finland, Poland, Scotland and Ireland. The species are closely related and interbreed where the forms meet, but most Hooded Crows are very different in appearance from Carrion Crows, with their frosty grey nape, mantle and breast. Hooded Crows are often tamer than Carrion Crows in towns and cities, but there are few other obvious differences in lifestyle. In common with the Carrion Crow, the Hoodie has a remarkable adaptability and will eat almost anything, although dead meat is always appreciated. It does not baulk at sifting through human rubbish; in fact, it relishes it, a session of garbage-checking being enough to make its day. Both Carrion and Hooded Crows are frequent robbers, both of their species and others, such as gulls. This species is exceptionally hardy and occurs right up into the Arctic Circle.

smart black and smoky-grey plumage

The Hooded Crow has a classic crow shape, with heavy bill and strong legs and feet, and flies with slow, steady wingbeats. **ADULT** Dapper with its overall smoky-grey plumage and contrasting black wings, tail, head and throat. Hybrids occur with the Carrion Crow that look messy. **VOICE** Gives a typical loud *caw*, often in threes. Not much different from that of the Carrion Crow. **MIGRATION** Mainly resident.

 BREEDING April–May, one brood. **NEST** Bulky platform of sticks, placed in a tree, or on a building, cliff ledge or pylon. **EGGS** 4–6, incubated for 18–20 days by female. **YOUNG** Leave nest at 4–5 weeks.

Crows are among the most intelligent of all birds – indeed, of all animals.

FACT FILE

FAMILY Corvidae (Crows). SIZE Length 44–51cm. Wingspan 85–90cm. FOOD Eats almost anything, especially meat. SIMILAR SPECIES Rook (p. 64) and Jackdaw (p. 58). The Carrion Crow has an identical shape.

CARRION CROW

Corvus corone

Generally abundant and ubiquitous.

This is an inky-black, furtive, seemingly sinister garden character with a voice as harsh as a sergeant-major. Highly suspicious of people, and usually shy, it is nonetheless very common in towns, cities, villages and gardens, and lives among us with great success. It is naturally hard to love, with its habit of feeding on carcasses and sometimes live animals, from birds to mammals to frogs and beetles. However, in most gardens, its intelligence is second only to the human inhabitants. Carrion Crows nest as pairs, not in colonies like Rooks (p. 64) – hence the term 'crow's nest'; however, in contrast to what many people think, they do readily form flocks and groups.

The all-black plumage, shifty gait and slow wingbeats give Carrion Crows something of a funereal, untrustworthy, sinister appearance.

The bill is thick and sunk well into the flat crown (see Rook), and the feathers on the belly are not baggy, but tighter fitting. It also hops on the ground if in a hurry, like a vulture. A public-relations firm would have its work cut out to make some of us love it. **ADULT** All-black plumage (not as glossy as a Rook's), including dark bill. **JUVENILE** Not obviously different from adult. **VOICE** Famous 'angry' *caw*. Often gives three calls in assertive series, as if it has got out of the wrong side of the bed. **MIGRATION** Resident.

FACT FILE

FAMILY Corvidae (Crows). Length 30–34cm. Wingspan 70–75cm. **FOOD** Omnivorous, taking huge variety of foods, from roadkill to grain. May store food. **SIMILAR SPECIES** Rook (especially juvenile) and Jackdaw (p. 58). The Hooded Crow (p. 60) has an identical shape. The Raven (*Corvus corax*) is very unusual in gardens, although it might fly over them. People often think they have Ravens in the garden because Carrions Crows look unexpectedly huge close up. A Raven, though, is the size of a Buzzard (p. 34), and has a massive bill and often a 'beard'. Its long wings and wedge-shaped tail are obvious in flight.

flat crown

heavy, dark bill

black plumage

BREEDING April–May, one brood. **NEST** Usually placed high in a tree and is a bulky platform of sticks, with four layers of different sizes of stick or twig. It is often buffeted by the wind. **EGGS** 4–6, incubated for 18–20 days by female. **YOUNG** Leave nest at 4–5 weeks.

In somewhat sinister fashion, a pair's space is sometimes infiltrated by a 'third bird', a young male interloper that is somehow tolerated. It is there to take its chance at pairing when the male dies.

The Carrion Crow will use your garden, invited or not. It likes ponds, in which it can moisten food before eating it.

ROOK

Corvus frugilegus

At heart a rural bird – abundant where fields and woods intermix – but also in towns.

In some ways the acceptable face of 'crow-dom', the Rook is a very different character from its more suspicious, territorial relative, living an intensely sociable life, rarely separated from others of its kind, reproducing in cheerful treetop colonies, and is lively and sunny. It is essentially a bird of the farming environment, foraging on arable fields and doing a superb job of consuming many of the invertebrates that farmers dislike, as well as worms and vegetable matter. Needing tall trees for its nests, it is comfortable settling near villages and often forms a noisy, but not annoying, backdrop to the early spring and summer atmosphere. It famously breeds early, even bringing sticks to refurbish its nest in January, an uplifting sign of spring on short, cold days. It is a common sight in and around rural gardens, but rarely thrives in suburbia except on the edge, and not in large cities.

dirty-white base to bill

peaked crown

glossy plumage

baggy feathers on thigh

Very similar to a Carrion Crow (p. 62), and the same size, the Rook has a distinctly different shape: while the Carrion Crow has a flat forehead into which the bill is sunk, the Rook has a narrow bill that makes a steep angle to the peaked forehead. Loose feathering on the belly makes it look as though it is wearing baggy shorts, as opposed to the leggings of the Carrion Crow. **ADULT** Easily told from the Carrion Crow by its dirty-white bill-base. **JUVENILE** Seen in summer. Lacks white bill and is very difficult to tell from a Carrion Crow. **VOICE** Call a *caw* similar to a Carrion Crow's but without all the fury. Rather than angry, ferocious *caw*s, often delivered in a sequence of three, it will give the odd one, and each call lacks the 'edge' of a Carrion Crow volley. It is as if a Rook was a Carrion Crow after anger-management classes. All manner of odd calls, including some that are quite high pitched, emanate from busy Rook colonies (rookeries). **MIGRATION** Mainly resident, but Scottish birds may evacuate the mountains in winter.

 BREEDING Breeds early, March–June, one brood. **NEST** Large platform of sticks, moulded together with earth, placed in a tall tree. Almost always in noisy colonies called rookeries. **EGGS** 3–4, incubated for 16–18 days. **YOUNG** Leave nest after 32–34 days, and travel around with the adults for a while, begging for food.

 In Hungary there was once a rookery with 16,000 pairs.

The birds pair up in autumn to allow for a quick start to breeding in spring.

FACT FILE

FAMILY Corvidae (Crows). SIZE Length 41–49cm. Wingspan 80–90cm. FOOD Omnivorous but worms and grain crucial. SIMILAR SPECIES Carrion Crow and Jackdaw (p. 58).

LONG-TAILED TIT

Aegithalos caudatus

Fairly common but easily overlooked in woods, scrub and gardens.

A tiny pink bird bursting with character, the Long-tailed Tit is one of the easiest birds to identify in the garden. It also comes in flocks, with numbers ranging from five to 12, sometimes more. All the birds arrive at once, occupy feeders or trees and shrubs for a while, then move on restlessly, never staying long, like visiting royalty. They are unique in shape, with the long tail used as a counterbalance in the shrubbery, allowing them to feed upside down, or in any posture. Although Long-tailed Tits take small seeds at feeders, they live all year round on insects, frequently taking items as small as butterfly eggs and aphids, and somehow that is enough for them to survive. The flocks are unique, composed as they are of family members. The birds you see together are parents and children, sometimes with uncles and aunts, too.

The unique combination of a long tail and very small body size readily identifies a Long-tailed Tit. The flight looks very weak, with fast

unique pink plumage

long tail

tiny

FACT FILE

FAMILY Aegithalidae (Long-tailed Tits). SIZE Length 13–15cm (tail 7–9cm). FOOD Small invertebrates, seeds. SIMILAR SPECIES At a stretch, Pied Wagtail (p. 134) but this bird is not usually in trees or bushes.

wingbeats and feeble undulations. **ADULT** Has a dark stripe that begins behind the eye and broadens to join the shoulders; distinctly pink tinged. **ADULT** (northern, Scandinavia): pure white head. **JUVENILE** Most of sides of face sooty; lacks pink tones. **VOICE** Three distinct calls, but the easiest to hear is a far-carrying, insistent *see-see-see* or *see-see-see-see*, uttered constantly by flock members. At close range gives a conversational *tupp*. Also heard is a curious spluttering, as if the bird is shocked while drinking tea. **MIGRATION** Resident.

BREEDING March–June, one brood. **NEST** Placed low down in a thorny bush, occasionally high in a tree fork. It is an astonishing dome of moss bound together with cobwebs, stuffed with feathers for insulation and with lichen on the outside. It takes both birds three weeks to build. **EGGS** 6–10, incubated for 12–14 days by female, fed by male. **YOUNG** Fed by both parents and, in many nests, by extra helpers (relatives). They leave at 14–18 days, then are still fed for 14 more days.

★ The Long-tailed Tit stuffs the inside of its nest with sometimes more than 1,000 feathers. Some of these are plucked from the corpses of recently dead birds.

★ Families of Long-tailed Tits huddle together horizontally on a perch on winter nights for warmth. The adults take the warmest positions in the middle and the young are positioned on the outside.

| JAN | FEB | MAR | APR | MAY | JUN | JUL | AUG | SEP | OCT | NOV | DEC |

BLUE TIT

Cyanistes caeruleus

Common throughout its range and present in most gardens.

Who says temperate birds are dull and colourless? No one told the Blue Tit. Due to its status as one of the most abundant garden birds throughout northern Europe, it is easy to overlook its stunning metallic blue wash and brilliant yellow underside. The birds do not overlook these features, since the intensity of the yellow and the ultraviolet light reflection from the blue are used for sexual selection. This is a cheery, bold, noisy and brash species that punches above its weight at birdfeeders. The strong legs and feet enable it to hang upside down and generally be acrobatic, especially up in the treetops, its natural home. In autumn and winter it is highly

cobalt-blue head and thin stripe through eyes

line down middle of breast less defined than Great Tit's

ABOVE: *JUVENILE*

sociable, often moving around in flocks. It habitually takes to any feeder going, but relishes hanging feeders especially, in which small-grain mixes should be used. Readily takes to nest-boxes.

The Blue Tit is much smaller than the Great Tit (p. 70), but the colour scheme is similar. **ADULT** Cobalt-blue cap and thin stripe through eye. There is often a narrow dark line down the middle of the breast, as if it liked the Great Tit's fashion but only adopted it half-heartedly. **JUVENILE** Similar to adult, but cheek is washed yellow and it often looks dishevelled and unfinished. **VOICE** Makes a bewildering variety of silvery phrases, the best known has three slow notes followed by a trill. It is a tough song to learn. Calls are equally confusing. Often makes a long-winded scold, seemingly over the top. **MIGRATION** Not a great migrant. Juveniles move around in summer.

BREEDING April–June. Almost always a single brood (breeding timed to coincide with glut of caterpillars.) **NEST** Hidden away in a nest-box or tree-hole, and sometimes in other natural holes – a relatively neat cup of moss. **EGGS** 8–10, incubated for two weeks. **YOUNG** Remain in nest for 18–21 days, longer than most small bird species. Fed by both parents on up to 1,000 caterpillars a day.

Intensity of yellow on breast is related to a bird's competence at catching caterpillars (the insects provide the pigment, via plant juices).

FACT FILE

FAMILY Paridae (Tits). SIZE Length 10.5–12cm. FOOD Caterpillars, seeds, nuts, insects.
SIMILAR SPECIES Great Tit, and perhaps Coal Tit (p. 74).

GREAT TIT

Parus major

Abundant woodland and garden bird; hardier than Blue Tit.

There will barely be a single garden in the whole of the region, indeed the whole of continental Europe, which has not had a visit from the ubiquitous Great Tit. One of the region's most successful birds, it seems to master every area and virtually every habitat, from the depths of remote forests to the most urban of gardens. It can seemingly do everything, from foraging in the treetops to feeding on the ground, and it acrobatically holds on to feeders using its powerful legs and feet. Its range of foods includes many garden invertebrates and seeds, and it is able to use its sense of smell to detect

big, with bold colouration

black crown, white cheeks

neat black stripe down breast

FACT FILE

FAMILY Paridae (Tits). SIZE Length 13.5–15cm. FOOD In summer insects, especially caterpillars; in autumn and winter seeds and nuts. SIMILAR SPECIES Blue Tit (p. 68); the Coal Tit (p. 74) looks like a smaller, monochromatic version.

insect larvae; it sometimes eats unusual foods, even bats. It is gorgeously colourful, aggressive, noisy and unstoppable – truly one of the garden's characters.

Big for a tit, the Great Tit is the size of a Chaffinch (p. 140). It flies strongly, with undulations. **ADULT** Easily identified by the bright yellow breast with a bold black stripe bisecting it; also by the white cheek surrounded by black. White outer-tail feathers. **MALE** Broader black stripe than female, reaching well down to the legs. The broadness varies between males. **FEMALE** Narrower, less well-defined black stripe. **JUVENILE** Yellow cheeks and sooty cap. **VOICE** Perhaps the sound of late winter, starting at Christmas. It is a loud, cheerful, ringing *TEE-cher, TEE-cher, TEE-cher...* song, repeated up to 3–6 times. The first note is quite harsh. Altogether it sounds like a foot pump. There is much variation in tone and speed – indeed, each male has at least three songs. It has a bewildering variety of calls. Perhaps most common are a *pink-pink* lacking the strength of the Chaffinch's similar call, and a short scold. However, it is not easy to recognize the call. **MIGRATION** Mainly resident.

ABOVE: *FEMALE (NARROWER BREAST STRIPE THAN THAT OF MALE)*

 BREEDING April–June, one brood, occasionally two. **NEST** Placed inside a hole, usually in a tree, but also in a building or even a squirrel drey. Cup of moss, hair and cobwebs. **EGGS** 8–13, incubated by female, fed by male, for 13–15 days. **YOUNG** Fed on caterpillars; adult often breaks jaw of larger ones before passing them on. Young leave nest at 16–22 days.

★ Birds brought up in conifers have a slightly different song from those brought up in a better habitat, such as broadleaved woodland.

★ A Great Tit can eat 44 per cent of its entire weight of seeds on a cold winter's day.

| JAN | FEB | MAR | APR | MAY | JUN | JUL | AUG | SEP | OCT | NOV | DEC |

CRESTED TIT

Lophophanes cristatus

Very localized, mainly near stands of old conifers.

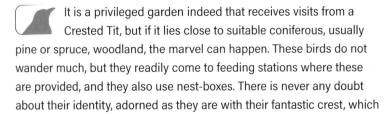

It is a privileged garden indeed that receives visits from a Crested Tit, but if it lies close to suitable coniferous, usually pine or spruce, woodland, the marvel can happen. These birds do not wander much, but they readily come to feeding stations where these are provided, and they also use nest-boxes. There is never any doubt about their identity, adorned as they are with their fantastic crest, which

they manage to make look fashionable – albeit sometimes giving the impression they have just been swimming. This is a very small tit that feeds at all levels, from the ground to the treetops, and differs from most tits in being extremely quiet. Its song does not descend from every treetop but is given sparingly.

This is the only very small garden bird with an obvious crest (other birds may raise their crown, but it is not a permanent feature). It flies with weak undulation. **ADULT** Well turned-out, smart tit with brown wings lacking any white bars; paler underneath. The crest is black with white chevrons and there is a black ear-crescent. **JUVENILE** Lacks the well-

perky crest

developed crest. **VOICE** The call and song are pretty much the same, a very distinctive bubbling, preceded by *si-si* notes, so *si-si-purrrrup* ('squeak and bubble'). **MIGRATION** Resident.

BREEDING April–June, one brood. **NEST** Female excavates its own nest-hole in a rotten tree stump or dead tree; the nest within is a cup of moss and lichen, with a lining of hair. **EGGS** 4–8, incubated by hard-working female for 13–16 days. **YOUNG** Fed only by male for first week, then both parents. Young fledge at 17–21 days.

In common with other brown tits, the Crested Tit stores food away for a rainy day, in this species in bark fissures, clumps of lichen and other hiding places. It stores caterpillars and spiders, having first paralysed them by biting their heads off.

FACT FILE

FAMILY Paridae (Tits). SIZE Length 10.5–12cm. FOOD Insects and their larvae in summer, seeds and nuts in winter. SIMILAR SPECIES Coal Tit (p. 74), Marsh Tit (p. 76) and Willow Tit (p. 78).

COAL TIT

Periparus ater

Common; especially associated with conifers.

The Coal Tit is famous for being bullied by other tits at feeders, but make no mistake, this is a supremely successful and adaptable species, with some unexpected spice in its lifestyle. It is one of the garden's smallest birds and has a habit of making flying visits to feeders, dashing in, grabbing a nut or seed, then sprinting away as fast as possible, often quite a distance away. An important thing to remember about Coal Tits is that they are mainly associated with conifer trees, and gardens with these are most likely to host them, particularly in the breeding season. This is slightly different in winter when the birds wander more, but it is a useful rule of thumb. Coal Tits are very small bodied and are the only small birds, other than Goldcrests (p. 94), that you might spot hovering up in the treetops. They have thinner bills than other tits and are able to reach among conifer needles, which helps them survive the winter.

This is a very small tit with a rather large head and short, pointy tail. It is often in the tops of conifer trees. **ADULT** Told from other tits by a unique combination of white wing-bars and brown plumage. There is also a distinctive white patch on the nape. Birds on the Continent have bluish-grey backs.

FACT FILE

FAMILY Paridae (Tits). SIZE Length 10–11.5cm. FOOD Insects and seeds. SIMILAR SPECIES Great Tit is larger but has similar head pattern; also Marsh Tit (p. 76), Willow Tit (p. 78) and Crested Tit (p. 72).

white patch on nape

grey-brown above, buff below

two white wing-bars

JUVENILE Similar to adult, but there is a yellow wash to the plumage, especially the cheeks. **VOICE** The song has the same pattern as that of a Great Tit (p. 70) – a see-sawing phrase like *teacher* repeated 3–5 times. However, it is softer than that of the Great Tit, without the harsh first note, and is sweet rather than cheerful. It can sound like a bicycle pump (the Great Tit sounds like a foot pump). The most common call is a far-carrying *dwee!* often heard endlessly from the tops of conifers. **MIGRATION** Mainly resident, although some northern populations move south a short distance for the winter.

BREEDING April–June; in contrast to other tits, sometimes has two broods, not just one. **NEST** In a hole, usually in a tree, but even among roots on the ground at times. Usual mossy cup typical of tits. **EGGS** 7–10, incubated by female, and fed by male for 14–16 days. **YOUNG** Leave at 16–19 days.

Coal Tits are extraordinarily unfaithful to their mates – about 25 per cent of all young are sired by a male other than the nurturing father of the brood.

MARSH TIT

Poecile palustris

Localized and fairly common, mostly near deciduous woodland.

What the Marsh Tit lacks in bright colour it makes up for in sheer smartness of attire. With its clean, brown plumage, paler below, and sharply defined, glossy black cap and black bib, it perfectly fits the upmarket dress code. It is also a self-effacing, quiet species although, from a birdwatcher's point of view, a slippery one. Although a regular garden bird, it is also highly localized and confined to mature deciduous woodland and nearby gardens – its English name is annoyingly wrong. Throughout its range, it invites the most complete confusion with the Willow Tit (p. 78), and many people find the two impossible to tell apart. The Marsh Tit's sneezing *pitch-oo* call is the best way, but it does not always make a sound when visiting feeders.

This is a small tit with sober plumage, neatly proportioned with a relatively small head and slim appearance (see Willow Tit). **ADULT** The black head and bib, combined with brown plumage without any white wing-bars, is shared by the almost identical Willow Tit. Look for the following: black cap is glossy, black bib is poorly defined, no hint of a pale wing-panel, white cheek well defined, evenly sized head. **VOICE** Shares the repetition of two notes with Great and Coal Tits (pp. 70 and

plain wings

glossy cap

74), but the first note is clipped. Sounds like working a pair of shears. The call is a distinctive *pit-chou*, with a sneezing quality ('caught cold in a marsh'). **MIGRATION** Non-migratory.

BREEDING April–June, one brood. **NEST** In a hole or cavity, usually a tree-hole (pre-existing, see Willow Tit.) Nest is a cup of moss lined with animal hair or feathers. **EGGS** 6–9, incubated for 14–16 days. **YOUNG** Leave nest at 17–19 days.

Extraordinarily flexible as to when it starts breeding. The first egg can be laid as much as 23 days earlier or later between years, depending on the weather.

FACT FILE

FAMILY Paridae (Tits). SIZE Length 11.5–13cm. FOOD Like other tits, insects in summer and seeds and nuts in autumn and winter. Also partial to berries. SIMILAR SPECIES Willow Tit and Coal Tit.

WILLOW TIT

Poecile montanus

Uncommon in south, but more common towards north, especially in coniferous forest belt.

This is a common tit in the northern forests of much of Scandinavia, where it is a regular garden bird. In the UK and nearby Continent its appearance is much patchier, and it occurs in a bewilderingly wide range of different habitats and is not particularly common in any of them – these include hedgerows, wetlands and birch woods as well as conifers. It shares the Marsh Tit's (p. 76) habit of being rather quiet, certainly lacking the overbearing nature of Blue and Great Tits (pp. 68 and 70). However, its nasal, buzzing call, often rendered *zi zi – char, char, char* is easily recognized. In common with the Marsh Tit,

broad head, matt black cap

FACT FILE

FAMILY Paridae (Tits). SIZE Length 12–13cm. FOOD Insects in summer, seeds through much of the year. SIMILAR SPECIES Marsh Tit and Coal Tit (p. 74).

it is far less sociable than other tits, which may almost swarm around feeders, and is usually only seen in ones and twos.

This is a smart brown tit with a slightly different shape from that of the Marsh Tit, with a larger head and nape, and slightly fluffier plumage. **ADULT** Subtle distinctions from the Marsh Tit include: matt-black cap, broader black on throat that is better defined, flanks sometimes warmer buff, more white on cheeks. **VOICE** Call a distinctive buzzing *chair, chair, chair,* often with short introduction, *si-si-chair, chair, chair.* Song, rarely heard, is *tsew-tsew-tsew...* **MIGRATION** Resident.

BREEDING April–June, one brood. **NEST** Made inside a hole excavated by female in a rotten tree stump or wooden post; nest itself is unusual for a tit in being made from wood chippings, not moss. **EGGS** 6–9, incubated by female, fed by male, for 13–15 days. **YOUNG** Stay in nest for 17–19 days, a long time for a small bird.

★ Has been recorded in breeding season at all altitudes between sea level and 4,000m (China).

| JAN | FEB | MAR | APR | **MAY** | **JUN** | **JUL** | **AUG** | SEP | OCT | NOV | DEC |

SWIFT

Apus apus

Common bird of summer skies; can be seen anywhere.

The definitive summer bird, the Swift arrives in May to ply the skies for flying insects, sweeping through the heavy lanes of invertebrate traffic congesting the upper airspace, above rooftop height. If it is not summer, and it is not in the sky, it is not a Swift. This curious bird never perches – it cannot, not on a wire, or on anything else. It can scramble into crevices, often in a church tower or other tall building, but otherwise does not touch down at all, often not for months on end. Parties of Swifts often fly in formation, like feathered jet fighters, perhaps careening around tall buildings, or even dashing over streets and squares, screaming in unison. The strangled squeal is another gorgeous evocation of warm weather and long days. On rainy or cloudy days it tends to feed over water, often very low down, feeding on just-hatched flying insects. It is then that you can tell how much larger and more powerful it is than a Swallow (p. 84) or House Martin (p. 82).

Always flying, the Swift shares the skies with Swallows and House Martins but is the most extreme in appearance, with narrow, pointed, scythe-like wings – look especially where the wing joins the body. It is faster and given to long sweeps across the sky, with uneven flaps of the wings. **ADULT** Plumage is largely dark brown, although it often looks black. There is a small patch of white on the chin. **VOICE** A screaming squeal. **MIGRATION** Very long-distance migrant first to tropical West Africa, and to forests of Central Africa, with some birds even reaching the coast of the Indian Ocean.

BREEDING May–July, one brood. Colonial. **NEST** The nest is a cup of fragments of vegetation caught on the wind and snatched by the bird, bound together with the Swift's saliva. The nests are in cavities in cliffs and tall buildings such as churches. **EGGS** 2–3, laid at two-day intervals, so young in nest are of different ages. Incubated for 19–20 days. **YOUNG** Fed by both parents for between 5 and 8 weeks, depending on food supply.

narrow wings

sickle-shaped wings

black body

⭐ Some birds, below the age of breeding, arrive in European airspace in May and stay until August, but their feet never touch the ground at all.

⭐ Swifts are known to sleep on the wing, and at times they do it on one side of the brain at a time – so while one hemisphere is active, the other is resting. This is known as unihemispheric slow-wave sleep.

⭐ When a weather front approaches, bringing bad weather, Swifts may simply evacuate the area and fly all around the front. They may fly 2,000km, even while their young are in the nest.

FACT FILE

FAMILY Apodidae (Swifts). SIZE Length 17–18.5cm. Wingspan 40–44cm. FOOD Flying insects, airborne spiderlings. SIMILAR SPECIES Swallow and House Martin.

| JAN | FEB | MAR | **APR** | **MAY** | **JUN** | **JUL** | **AUG** | **SEP** | **OCT** | NOV | DEC |

HOUSE MARTIN

Delichon urbicum

Common but declining summer visitor, often to towns and villages.

Often confused with the Swallow (p. 84), the House Martin has adopted a similar lifestyle of spending most of its time airborne, foraging on summer's bounty of flying insects. However, while the Swallow eats relatively large insects, such as blowflies, low down and close to the ground, the House Martin feeds on smaller flying insects higher up, above the rooftops. It is famous for its nests, which are amazing cup-shaped structures built at the tops of vertical walls, often against the eaves of buildings. The nests are made up from hundreds of pellets of mud, and the birds are often seen collecting mud from puddles. The birds usually nest in colonies, and these can provide wonderful entertainment where they are built in suburban or even urban locations. In common with the Swallow, the House Martin is a summer visitor, welcomed with delight in April and leaving in October. It has a very long breeding season, and the last chicks may begin October still in the nest.

snowy-white underneath, including throat

FACT FILE

FAMILY Hirundinidae (Swallows and Martins). SIZE Length 13.5–15cm. Wingspan 26–29cm. FOOD Flying insects, mostly small, such as aphids and ants. SIMILAR SPECIES Swallow and Swift.

short tail with shallow fork

ABOVE: *WHITE RUMP*

FAR LEFT: *JUVENILE*

BELOW: *AT NEST*

The House Martin looks similar to the Swallow but with a shorter tail, with a much shallower fork. It flies in a different way – more circumspect, with more turns and arcs in the sky – and is more fluttery. It also flies higher up. **ADULT** Easily distinguished from a Swallow or Swift by white rump. It is entirely snowy-white underneath and dark blue-black above. **JUVENILE** Dirtier underside. **VOICE** Song a series of calls with cheeps, usually heard at the nest. Call a short, flatulent rasp. **MIGRATION** Long-distance migrant to Africa, but precisely where is not known yet.

 BREEDING May–October, two broods (occasionally three), usually in colonies. **NEST** Cup stuck to a vertical wall or rock face, flush to a roof, eave or overhang, to leave a narrow entrance at the top. Made from mud pellets and plant fibres and lined with feathers. **EGGS** 4–5, incubated for 14–16 days. **YOUNG** Fed by both parents on flying insects for about 15 days, after which the parents try to lure them out by withholding food.

The winter quarters of House Martins are unknown.

| JAN | FEB | **MAR** | **APR** | **MAY** | **JUN** | **JUL** | **AUG** | **SEP** | **OCT** | NOV | DEC |

SWALLOW

Hirundo rustica

Very common summer visitor; avoids urban areas.

One of Britain's most popular birds, the Swallow is the harbinger of spring, its appearance after a long winter a sight to lift the spirits. Its marathon flight to and from southern Africa is truly one of nature's marvels. This is a bird of the air, which flits and skips effortlessly low over fields and other open areas, plying the warm drafts of summer for flying insects, which it snaps up in its bill, one by one. It is also a perky dweller on wires and other perches, making pleasing conversational twitters, as if discussing the gossip. As a breeding bird it prefers rural areas, especially older settlements and farmsteads, nesting on the inner eaves of barns, often in close proximity to people and their livestock. On migration there is scarcely anywhere that has not been covered by the shadow of this long-distance traveller. Its stay in the region is longer than many people realize; it is not at

RIGHT: *AT NEST*

rust-coloured throat

buff below

forked tail

all unusual to still see Swallows around in mid-October.

The species is easily recognized by its relatively broad wing-bases (compared with the Swift, p. 80) and its long tail-streamers (compared with the House Martin, p. 82). **ADULT** Buff belly (pale, unlike in Swift), dark breast-band and red face (unlike House Martin). Bottle-blue, with white marks on tail. **MALE** Longer tail than female or juvenile. **JUVENILE** Pale not red face. **VOICE** Song is a delightful, lively twitter, often given from a wire or perch near nest. Every so often male adds strange buzzing sounds. Call is a cheery *wit, wit*. **MIGRATION** To southern Africa, moving by day.

 BREEDING April–August, 2–3 broods. **NEST** Usually inside a building such as a barn or shed. Cup of mud pellets, strengthened with grass or other fragments of vegetation, lined with feathers and often placed on beam or rafter and up against roof. **EGGS** 4–5, incubated for 14–16 days. **YOUNG** Leave nest after 17–24 days, but initially return to roost in nest each night.

 Females preferentially choose males with longer tails, and with even-length tail-streamers.

Unpaired male Swallows occasionally kill the chicks of a pair and get together with the female whose offspring they have murdered.

FACT FILE

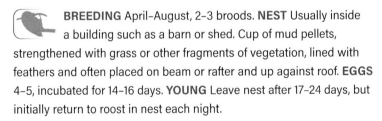

FAMILY Hirundinidae (Swallows and Martins). SIZE Length 17–21cm (including tail). Wingspan 29–32cm. FOOD Mainly flying insects, especially chunky ones such as large flies and bees. SIMILAR SPECIES House Martin and Swift.

| JAN | FEB | MAR | **APR** | **MAY** | **JUN** | **JUL** | **AUG** | **SEP** | OCT | NOV | DEC |

WILLOW WARBLER

Phylloscopus trochilus

Common, often abundant summer visitor to bushy areas and woodland edges, especially in north.

As a garden bird, the Willow Warbler is mainly a northern species, familiar in Scotland and Scandinavia, for example, where in spring its lovely, delicate song seems to trickle down from every tree. It is one of those garden birds that has no connection with humans – it comes neither to our feeding stations, nor our nest-boxes, and it does not benefit much from what we plant. If we ceased to exist, it would barely notice. It is a bird of the trees that is very easy to miss, as it is small, green and busy, hidden behind a layer of leaves. Most garden enthusiasts are likely to see it in spring or, especially, autumn, when migrant individuals touch down almost anywhere for a quick

BELOW: *ADULT SPRING*

yellow eyebrow

pale cheeks

FACT FILE

FAMILY Phylloscopidae (Leaf Warblers). SIZE Length 11–12.5cm. FOOD Various invertebrates; a few berries before migration. SIMILAR SPECIES Chiffchaff. The Icterine Warbler (*Hippolais icterina*) is found in some continental gardens. It is larger and more sluggish than the Willow Warbler, and lacks an eye-stripe.

feed and brush-up. It is typical among warblers for being restless and twitchy, moving rapidly in the foliage, flitting about and examining the vegetation for insects.

ABOVE: *ADULT SUMMER*

LEFT: *JUVENILE AUTUMN*

This is a small, dynamic, restless bird that rarely stays still, with modest pale green plumage. It is one of two famously similar species, the other being the Chiffchaff (p. 88). It has a flatter head and longer wings. It does not continually wag its tail but does flick it from time to time (see Chiffchaff). **ADULT** Neater and often brighter than Chiffchaff, with yellower eyebrow and paler cheeks, so the eye-ring is not visible. The legs are pale. **JUVENILE** Fairly bright yellow. **VOICE** Song a beautiful, understated, wispy descending scale, almost blown away on the wind. Call is *hooet*, like that of the Chiffchaff but gentler and clearly of two syllables. **MIGRATION** Long-distance migrant to tropical Africa.

 BREEDING April–July, 1–2 broods. **NEST** Rarely nests in gardens. Nest is a dome of grass, moss and leaves, with a side entrance, placed in a concealed position on the ground, often under a bush or hedge. **EGGS** 4–8, incubated for 13 days by female. **YOUNG** Fed by both parents, and fledge at 13–16 days.

★ Exceptionally aggressive in defence of its territory. Fights to the death between males are well known.

JAN | FEB | **MAR** | **APR** | **MAY** | **JUN** | **JUL** | **AUG** | **SEP** | **OCT** | NOV | DEC

CHIFFCHAFF

Phylloscopus collybita

Common woodland summer visitor; some individuals overwinter.

An effervescent, olive-green force of nature, the Chiffchaff should be a great favourite of garden enthusiasts, but it is small, lacks much colour and keeps itself to itself. Like the Willow Warbler (p. 86), it keeps hidden in the vegetation and flits about its business, but it does sometimes use a bird bath and join flocks of other birds, especially in summer. In Britain it is a very common woodland bird and tends to visit gardens after breeding, or on migration. Throughout the region it is found in gardens with tall deciduous trees. It is famously very difficult to tell apart from the Willow Warbler, which looks almost identical. However, there is one excellent tip that usually works. When feeding, the Chiffchaff constantly flits its tail down, so much so that it looks like a nervous tic. The Willow Warbler only occasionally does this.

This Blue Tit-sized sprite with dull olive-green plumage, darker above and paler below, flits about restlessly. Look for the round head, small bill and short wings (see Willow Warbler). **ADULT** Look for the

obvious 'split' white eye-ring

short wings

dark legs

obvious pale eyebrow, and half eye-ring. The legs are dark. **JUVENILE** Looks yellower. **VOICE** Song a wondrously incessant repetition of notes sounding like *chiff* and *chaff*, usually in bouts of 8–15. The English name for it is a good description. It arrives in March, singing straightaway, and is one of the last birds to stop in summer, still chiffing and chaffing well into July. Call is a breathy, quite enthusiastic *hweet*! (compare to Willow Warbler.) Many other birds make a similar sound, so may be confusing. **MIGRATION** Many northern populations migrate a long way to tropical West Africa, but others only go to the Mediterranean.

BREEDING April–July, 1–2 broods. **NEST** Dome of dead leaves, grass and other vegetation, with a side entrance, placed above the ground in grass or rank vegetation. **EGGS** 5–6, incubated by female for 13–14 days. **YOUNG** Fed almost entirely by nest-building, incubating, provisioning single-parent female, and they fledge at 14–16 days.

Male and female Chiffchaffs have little in common, even after producing eggs. The female stays near the ground, and the male sings in the treetops.

FACT FILE

FAMILY Phylloscopidae (Leaf Warblers). **SIZE** Length 10–12cm. **FOOD** Almost entirely invertebrates. **SIMILAR SPECIES** Willow Warbler.

| JAN | FEB | MAR | APR | MAY | JUN | JUL | AUG | SEP | OCT | NOV | DEC |

BLACKCAP

Sylvia atricapilla

Mostly a summer visitor to many kinds of woodland; often in gardens in winter in south.

Most people see a Blackcap for the first time on their bird table or other feeders, where it has a reputation for being aggressive, chasing other birds away. However, it is also a very common species of woodland edges and can be found in many larger gardens as a breeding species during the summer. The Blackcap is quite sluggish for a small bird, especially when it is foraging in bushes, either for insects or for its favourite autumn tipple, berries. Its movements are heavy and ponderous, quite unlike those of many other garden visitors – not for it the wild ride of an acrobatic Blue Tit (p. 68) in the high branches. Blackcaps are not sociable, although you might have several individuals in a winter garden. Most birds in the region are long-distance migrants to West Africa, arriving in early April and leaving in September, but the winter birds in gardens in Britain and the Low Countries are a new cohort of northern and eastern birds that

black cap

distinctly greyish plumage

FACT FILE

FAMILY Sylviidae (Old World Warblers). SIZE Length 13.5–15cm. FOOD Mainly insects in summer, but switches to berries in autumn and winter. SIMILAR SPECIES Small brown birds such as the Robin (p. 120) and Dunnock (p. 130).

ABOVE: *FEMALE*

LEFT: *JUVENILE*

have evolved not to migrate so far.

The Blackcap is a greyish, small brown bird, if that makes sense. Surprisingly sluggish and stocky, and not at all feverish, it is generally well proportioned. **ADULT** Would be completely dull grey-brown except for the distinctive cap. **MALE** Black skullcap, which goes down to the eye. **FEMALE** Reddish-brown cap. **JUVENILE** Similar, browner. **VOICE** The lovely song is a cheerful but slightly aimless and tuneless whistle, of the sort you may hear from a visiting tone-deaf tradesperson mending your dishwasher. It starts hesitantly, then develops a strong, fluty flow. Call is *tack*, to go with *cap*, like two stones struck together. **MIGRATION** Northern populations go to West Africa, while those further south remain in Europe, for example in Spain.

 BREEDING April–July, 1–2 broods. **NEST** Male builds several partial nests and female chooses one. It is a rather neat cup of dry grass and roots placed in thick vegetation well above ground. **EGGS** 4–5, incubated for 10–15 days by both sexes. **YOUNG** Leave nest at 11–12 days, unable to fly properly for a day or two.

Birds from Central Europe used to migrate to Spain for the winter; now they go to Britain instead.

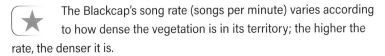

The Blackcap's song rate (songs per minute) varies according to how dense the vegetation is in its territory; the higher the rate, the denser it is.

| JAN | FEB | MAR | APR | MAY | JUN | JUL | AUG | SEP | OCT | NOV | DEC |

GARDEN WARBLER

Sylvia borin

Common summer visitor to the Continent, to scrubby areas; less common in UK.

The Garden Warbler is famous among birdwatchers for its remarkably featureless plumage – brown and nothing else. In a perverse way, this makes it quite easy to identify; in particular, the blank face with a dark eye is something of a giveaway. In Britain, it is not a common garden bird at all, despite the name; only the very largest and wildest gardens, with tall bushes, are likely to host it. In Scandinavia and parts of the east of the region, though, it is much more numerous. In common with the warblers in general it is a skulker, keeping inside the foliage of bushes or trees, and it is more difficult to see than the Blackcap (p. 90). In fact, it would probably pass the summer without being noticed if it was not for its golden voice – a wonderfully rich, effervescent, babbling song emanates from cover. In contrast to the Blackcap, it is a late migrant, arriving well into April, and it also leaves early and has largely vanished by the end of August.

This is a well-built and well-proportioned small brown bird with a staring dark eye and surprisingly short bill. **ADULT** Famously featureless, mouse-brown above, paler below, with hint of grey on nape. **VOICE** Song is a vivacious babble that flows evenly, of very similar

dark, staring eye

featureless
brown plumage

pitch and tone to the Blackcap's, but without the hesitant start, and less fluty. Call is a sort of *check*, not as sharp as the Blackcap's *tack*. **MIGRATION** Summer visitor: long-distance migrant to tropical West Africa south to Botswana.

BREEDING May–July and may squeeze in two broods, although it is usually one. **NEST** Selects a thick shrub, small tree or rank herbage, placing a scruffy cup of grasses 30cm–3m above ground; the male often builds several nest structures, which the female may line, or both start again. **EGGS** 4–5, incubated for 10–12 days by both adults. **YOUNG** Leave nest after 9–12 days.

Experiments have shown that the Garden Warbler's migration route is innately programmed. Caged birds try to fly off south in September but south-east in October, just as wild migrants do.

FACT FILE

FAMILY Sylviidae (Old World Warblers). **SIZE** Length 13–14.5cm. **FOOD** Invertebrates, some berries. **SIMILAR SPECIES** Small brown birds such as the Robin (p. 120) and Dunnock (p. 130).

| JAN | FEB | MAR | APR | MAY | JUN | JUL | AUG | SEP | OCT | NOV | DEC |

GOLDCREST

Regulus regulus

Easily overlooked resident, mainly around conifers, but also scrubby gardens in winter.

This is the smallest bird you will see in the garden – that is if you can see it at all. It is remarkably easy to overlook, due to its habit of incessantly and restlessly moving around – flitting, and hardly ever giving a decent view. It is also often in the treetops, especially in conifer trees, its natural home – the combination of dense needles and a tiny bird is challenging to see. If you do get a view of it, notice the podgy body, short tail, sharp bill and pale wing-bars. It is very difficult to see the famous crest. Occasionally, especially in winter, Goldcrests forage low down and can remain for some time in one shrub, giving wonderful, out-of-character views. These minute

BELOW: *FEMALE*

yellow crown-stripe (more orange in male)

FACT FILE

FAMILY Regulidae (Kinglets). SIZE Length 8.5–9.5cm. FOOD Invertebrates. SIMILAR SPECIES The Firecrest (*Regulus ignicapillus*) is very similar, but has a black stripe through its eye and bronze on the shoulder and is paler below.

birds, the smallest in Europe, occur in the region all year round, which is quite a feat in the cold of Scandinavia. Their small size and needle-thin bills allow them, appropriately enough, to forage amid the mini-forest of needles in the treetops.

In appearance, this is a minute, rotund treetop bird with a needle-like bill, never staying still and repeatedly nervously flicking its wings. **ADULT** Olive-green, paler below, with a staring dark eye giving a blank expression. Pale wing-bars and panels. **MALE** Some orange on yellow crown. **FEMALE** Yellow crown. **JUVENILE** Lacks crown. **VOICE** Song like the bird itself, needle sharp – a short, cyclical warble leading up to a finish (the finish may contain imitations of other birds.) Too high pitched for some people to hear. Call is a hissy *see-see-see* and variations. **MIGRATION** Mostly resident, but some northern populations migrate south, for example to Britain.

BREEDING April–July, two broods. **NEST** Remarkable nest is suspended from a fork or thin branch in a conifer, often high up. It is open purse shaped, made from moss and cobwebs, with lichen on the outside and stuffed with up to 2,500 feathers, some across the entrance. It is built by both sexes. **EGGS** 7–13, incubated for 16–19 days. Young fledge at 16–21 days, a long time for small birds.

In the north, while the female is incubating the first brood the male starts building a second nest. When the young hatch he then takes control of feeding the young while the female lays the second batch of eggs.

needle-thin bill

WREN

Troglodytes troglodytes

Abundant and noisy, although easily overlooked.

This is undoubtedly the most common garden bird that many people have never seen. There will be few gardens, or at least neighbourhoods, that do not have Wrens – perhaps the most urban ones are exceptions – but Wrens are so small and secretive that they are very difficult to see. They are not quite the smallest bird in the garden – that is the Goldcrest (p. 94), just. The problem is that Wrens spend most of their lives amid thick vegetation and hidden nooks and crannies, usually close to the ground, and they do not usually reveal their full selves. If you do spot one, you might think you are looking at a mouse, because the size and jerky motion recalls the rodent. The Wren is present in the garden all year round. If you know the song, you encounter it everywhere.

The Wren is unique, a very small, rotund ball of feathers with a short tail, which is usually held up vertically. It prefers vegetation close to ground level.

ADULT/JUVENILE The shape, plus the barred brown plumage, is distinctive. There is a noticeable pale streak over the eye. The thin bill is slightly downcurved.

VOICE Song is famous for being astonishingly loud for such a small bird. It is a long and fast phrase, often with a buzzy trill in the middle – you can imagine it being like an excited commentary on a 100m race. The phrase is repeated, but the

white eyebrow

short tail, often held upright

barred brown plumage

bird does not always sing it completely. The Wren sings all year round except for July, too, which is unusual. Any loud and prolonged song from low down in cover is likely to be that of a Wren. Call is a loud, somewhat irritable *tek!* This can be said multiple times in a machine-gun like rattle. Both calls are very frequent because the Wren is noisy. **MIGRATION** Resident.

 BREEDING April–July, two broods. **NEST** The male builds several half nests ('cock nests') for the female to inspect; she completes the inner furnishings of the one she chooses. The structure is domed, with a side entrance, is made up from moss, grass and leaves, and is placed in a crevice or hole low down. **EGGS** 5–8, incubated for 16 days. **YOUNG** Fledge at 15–20 days.

★ In very cold conditions several Wrens may pack into a small crevice or hole. However, the owner of the roost site has its favourites and does not let everyone in.

★ Young may roost in one of the male's half-built nests.

FACT FILE

FAMILY Troglodytidae (Wrens). SIZE Length 9–10.5cm. FOOD Small invertebrates. SIMILAR SPECIES None.

| JAN | FEB | MAR | APR | MAY | JUN | JUL | AUG | SEP | OCT | NOV | DEC |

NUTHATCH

Sitta europaea

A woodland bird (mainly deciduous); visits gardens with trees.

A feathered breath of fresh air, the Nuthatch is a distinctive and unusual bird that occurs in gardens near woods. Although it mainly lives in the treetops, it is very noisy, and cannot resist visiting feeders for nuts and seeds. The Nuthatch is adapted to creeping up and down tree trunks and branches, adhering closely to the bark, in similar mode to the Treecreeper (p. 100). However, most unusually, it is capable of creeping down head first as well as up head first, and you often see it clinging to a tree with its head down but facing outwards, and tail up, one foot above the other, as if it is about to dive off. It also feeds on the ground. It is a smart, well-turned-out bird, and has been aptly described as 'like a kingfisher that had dived into detergent and lost its lustre'. It is bold and relatively tame, and visits gardens all year round.

BELOW LEFT: *MALE*

BELOW RIGHT: *TYPICAL POSTURE ON TREE TRUNK*

FACT FILE

FAMILY Sittidae (Nuthatches). SIZE Length 12–14.5cm. FOOD Invertebrates, seeds and nuts. Often hordes nuts in autumn. SIMILAR SPECIES None.

blue above, buff below

sharp, chisel-shaped bill

This is a chubby, large-headed songbird with a long, sharp bill and short tail. It is usually seen clinging to a trunk or branch but will feed on the ground. The flight is very undulating, like a small woodpecker's. The bird is very active. **MALE** Blue-grey above, buff below, intensifying to chestnut on the flanks; black eye-stripe. **FEMALE** Paler on flanks than male. **VOICE** Song not well known, a sort of mewing of slurred whistling notes, quite wild sounding. Call is a loud, cheerful whistle, *chwit*, *chwit*, and multiple variations, including rapid-fire excitable bursts. Listen out also for steady tapping. Nuthatches lodge seeds in bark fissures and beat them. **MIGRATION** Resident, but in some years Scandinavian birds move south in numbers.

 BREEDING April–June, 1–2 broods. **NEST** In a hole, usually in a tree; the Nuthatch collects mud and plasters it around the entrance and often inside, to make it the correct size and keep bigger birds out. Nest itself is a cup of bark detritus and leaves. **EGGS** 6–8, incubated for 14–18 days. **YOUNG** Leave nest at 23–25 days.

⭐ On a winter's day, the Nuthatch spends 90 per cent of its time gathering food.

| JAN | FEB | MAR | APR | MAY | JUN | JUL | AUG | SEP | OCT | NOV | DEC |

TREECREEPER

Certhia familiaris

Secretive but common woodland bird, often visits wooded gardens but overlooked.

The Treecreeper is small and brown and lives up to its name by creeping up tree trunks. With head pointing up and tail down, it inches upwards with small hops, half-bird and half-mouse. It feeds on insects, using its long, curved bill to probe into crevices in the bark. Its long tail is stiffened to provide a brace, along with its sharp-clawed feet. When feeding, it starts at the bottom of a tree, works its way upwards, taking left and right turns and often describing a vague spiral, until it reaches the thin branches of the canopy, from where it flies down to the bottom of another tree. It is found in many wooded gardens, but is quiet and hard to spot, so easily overlooked.

The bird's shape and habits are unique, except for the almost identical Short-toed Treecreeper (opposite). Note the slim body, long tail and long, curved bill. **ADULT** Upperparts a mixture of brown dots, dashes, streaks and bars, perfectly imitating tree bark. Underparts are pure white (see Short-toed Treecreeper.) **VOICE** Song is a whisper, a phrase that lilts down the scale, rising at the end. Call is a sibilant whistle, *srri*, difficult to hear and identify. **MIGRATION** Resident.

BREEDING April–July, two broods. **NEST** Placed behind loose bark or crevice in a tree, or in a creeper such as ivy. Nest is a canoe-shaped loose cup of twigs, moss, cobwebs and grass. **EGGS** 5–6, incubated for 14 days. **YOUNG** Fledge at 14–16 days and immediately creep and climb on trunks like the adults, if a little gingerly.

A male sometimes pairs up with two females. Two nests have been recorded being built side by side, with a different female incubating in each.

long, curved bill

mouse-brown above, white below

FACT FILE

FAMILY Certhiidae (Treecreepers). SIZE Length 12.5–14cm. FOOD Insects and, in winter, small seeds. SIMILAR SPECIES Short-toed Treecreeper.

| JAN | FEB | MAR | APR | MAY | JUN | JUL | AUG | SEP | OCT | NOV | DEC |

SHORT-TOED TREECREEPER

Certhia brachydactyla

It is all but impossible to distinguish a Short-toed Treecreeper by sight from a Treecreeper (opposite). The most obvious difference is that the Short-toed Treecreeper is by far the noisier of the two; its songs and calls are conspicuous and far carrying. It also has a fractionally shorter hind-claw, and this disqualifies it from foraging easily on smooth-barked trees such as beech and some conifers. On the whole, it prefers gardens with broadleaved trees with rough bark. It creeps up tree trunks, close to the bark, in a series of hops. It is unusual in shape with a long, stiffened tail, mouse-like body and thin, curved bill. **ADULT** The Treecreeper is found in Britain, Scandinavia, the Baltic and mountains of Europe. The Short-toed Treecreeper occurs in the lowlands of continental Europe. In addition, the Short-toed Treecreeper has buffier, less pure white underparts, its eye-stripe begins behind its eye, it has a plain brown, not white-streaked forehead, and its 'staircase' wing-bar has even steps. **VOICE** Song is a pleasant, high-pitched phrase that does not go down and up the scale, and sounds quite confident. Call is a loud, penetrating *seeoo*. **MIGRATION** Resident.

Continental version of Treecreeper, noisier and easier to see.

BREEDING March–July, two broods. **NEST** Behind flaking bark. Delicate cup supported by twigs and made up from grass, roots and moss, and lined with feathers. **EGGS** 5–6, incubated for 14 days. **YOUNG** Fledge at 14–16 days.

In cold weather the birds frequently roost together in sheltered parts of a trunk, huddling their bodies together and often making a star shape.

dusky flanks

FACT FILE

FAMILY Certhiidae (Treecreepers). SIZE Length 13cm. FOOD Insects and, in winter, small seeds. SIMILAR SPECIES Treecreeper.

STARLING

Sturnus vulgaris

Often abundant in towns, cities and open country.

 You would not invite a group of Starlings to a genteel tea party – it is best that they stay out in the garden. These busy, bustling characters have a delightfully uncouth nature, being noisy, quarrelsome and with a tendency to wolf down their food – the latter habit is to help them eat quickly when dangerously out in the open. They are birds of grassland, and it happens that lawns, especially untreated, pesticide-free ones, make ideal foraging areas. Starlings eat many invertebrates that gardeners do not like, such as leatherjackets. Arriving in groups of 6–10, they walk over the ground with a confident, jaunty stride, like teenagers seeking to impress, and they use their spiky bills to make holes in the earth to detect food. Starlings often breed near houses, and perch on roofs and aerials. Here they produce a most unusual song, which sometimes sounds as though they are going through a dial to tune to random radio broadcasts.

BELOW: *NON-BREEDING ADULT (JULY-MARCH)*

oily black plumage with pale spots

spiky bill

This is a distinctive bird with unusual black, oily plumage, a spiky bill and a short tail. It is usually in small to large groups. In flight, the wings have a decidedly triangular shape. The wing feathers are pale edged. **ADULT** Spring and summer: black with a glossy-green tinge, purple in places. Winter: plumage covered with pale spots (the stars). **MALE** Yellow bill with blue base. **FEMALE** Yellow bill with pink base. **JUVENILE** Looks like a different species: unspotted, latte coloured, with dark bill and patch in front of eye. **VOICE** A hugely varied, rambling, rapid-fire demented song, full of whistles, buzzes and squeaks. Also imitates birds and other sounds (car alarms and so on). Call is a grating *tchick*, a common sound. Young make a curious hoarse *tscherr*, very much a sound of midsummer in gardens. **MIGRATION** Resident in Britain and near Continent, but northern and eastern populations are strongly migratory, moving south and west within Europe.

ABOVE: *ADULT MALE SUMMER*

LEFT: *GROUP*

BREEDING April–June, 1–2 broods. **NEST** In a hole or cavity, often a tree-hole, or in a drainpipe, brickwork, creeper, and so on. Nest is a mess of leaves and grasses made by the male before pairing, and completed by the female. **EGGS** 4–7, incubated for 12–15 days by both sexes. **YOUNG** Fledge at 20–22 days, but remain dependent for a while, shamelessly begging from the adults.

Male selects certain plants with aromatic properties for the nest.

Starlings are famous for their winter roosts, which can contain a million birds.

FACT FILE

FAMILY Sturnidae (Starlings). SIZE Length 19–22cm. Wingspan 35–40cm. FOOD Various invertebrates, plus berries in autumn. SIMILAR SPECIES The Blackbird (p. 106) is superficially similar but is usually alone.

| JAN | FEB | MAR | APR | MAY | JUN | JUL | AUG | SEP | OCT | NOV | DEC |

WAXWING

Bombycilla garrulus

Wandering, rare winter visitor to almost anywhere with berries.

The Waxwing is no ordinary bird. There are many garden enthusiasts who have planted berry-bearing shrubs in the express hope that, one day in the future, they might be visited by a flock of these exotic-looking visitors from the north. The birds will come to berry-bearing shrubs and trees in the garden, with favourites including cotoneaster. Over most of the region they are rare winter visitors, but due to their love of berries (they can eat 400 a day) when Waxwings are on the move they often turn up in unusual places, including suburbia and, famously, supermarket car parks, which often have berry-laden shrubs planted for landscaping. Waxwings eat berries all year, and if a good breeding season coincides with a poor autumn berry crop in northern Scandinavia, many more individuals than usual come south to look for food and spill down to Britain, France and the Low Countries. This movement is called an irruption, and only happens every few years. It is an event that birdwatchers look forward to with keen anticipation.

FACT FILE

FAMILY Bombycillidae (Waxwings). SIZE Length 18–21cm. FOOD Berries. SIMILAR SPECIES Flight is similar to that of a Starling, so flocks could be confused – not when the birds land, though.

wispy crest

unmistakable colouring

Waxwings are about the size of Starlings (p. 102), but easily distinguished by the fabulous crest. Their flight is also similar to the Starling's. **ADULT** Unmistakable, with its fluffy, pink-brown plumage, waxy wing-markings and fabulous made-up face. **YOUNG** First winter: do not have chevrons along the wing-tip, just a line. **VOICE** Makes a very distinctive, high-pitched trill call, like a bell used by fairies. **MIGRATION** Complicated. Birds leave northern forests to winter south, but how far they go depends on the berry crop. Different numbers each year find their way to Britain and the near Continent.

 BREEDING In the northern forests breeds very late (usually from mid-June) because it feeds its young on berries, which only become available then. One brood. **NEST** Fairly robust cup of sticks built in a conifer, usually by a swamp. **EGGS** 4–6, incubated by female, fed by male, for 14–15 days. **YOUNG** Remain in nest for 14–17 days.

 Sometimes catches snowflakes in flight, as if they were flying insects.

Waxwings are completely non-territorial, not even protecting the area around their nest.

JAN	FEB	MAR	APR	MAY	JUN	JUL	AUG	SEP	OCT	NOV	DEC

BLACKBIRD

Turdus merula

Extremely common bird of gardens, scrub and woodland.

Most of us know the Blackbird, a species that runs across the grass looking for worms. It has a familiar foraging method, standing still for a moment, then breaking into a run, standing still, maybe running off in a different direction, and so on. When it stops, it often holds its head slightly downwards, which helps it to both see and hear worms, insect larvae and other morsels. The Blackbird also feeds among dead leaves on the ground, shuffling with its feet, and making a rustling noise that sounds like a larger animal. Blackbirds are famously aggressive, and often chase each other and smaller birds, such as Song Thrushes (p. 108). They have a threatening posture, with plumage ruffled. In quiet moments they sometimes sunbathe on the grass or earth. They readily nest in garden shrubbery and have a long breeding season, sometimes consisting of three nesting attempts. A common experience is to hear 'angry' Blackbirds making their loud *chink* notes, which they do in the evening when settling down to roost. They make the same call when calling at a cat or owl.

This is a medium-sized, solidly built, long-tailed bird with strong legs and feet. It runs along lawns and often cocks its tail up, for example when alighting. It flies off low if alarmed. **MALE** Jet-black with orange-yellow bill. Young males have dark bills. **FEMALE** Mainly dark brown, though obviously streaked on the breast. Bill dull yellow. **JUVENILE**

BELOW: *FEMALE*

Gingery-brown and covered with pale spots. **VOICE** One of the loveliest of all garden bird songs, in tone quite close to a human whistle, delivered in effortless fashion, from a treetop or, especially, from a roof or aerial. The song phrases have significant pauses in between, and the pattern is that the phrases are not repeated, but each phrase is different from the last (see Song Thrush, p. 108). This song is a joy to listen to in February–July, often heard at dawn and dusk. Call is a friendly *chook*, an 'angry' *chink* especially at dusk, and a madcap panicky rattle when alarmed. **MIGRATION** Mostly resident,

jet black

yellow eye-ring

yellow bill

but birds from the north and east of the region migrate south within continental Europe, often in large numbers to Britain and France.

 BREEDING March–July, up to three broods. **NEST** Rather large, solid cup of thin twigs, roots, dead leaves and grass, with inner lining of mud and plant material, and inside that more soft grass and other material (see Song Thrush). It is placed in a bush or tree, in a fork. **EGGS** 4–5, incubated for about 14 days. **YOUNG** Fledge at 12–19 days.

⭐ The repertoire of the singing male Blackbird improves with age, and so does its prospect of pairing.

⭐ The intensity of yellow in a male Blackbird's bill is a reliable indicator of its state of health.

BELOW: *FLEDGLING*

FACT FILE

FAMILY Turdidae (Thrushes). **SIZE** Length 23.5–29cm. **FOOD** Many invertebrates, especially worms; berries in season. **SIMILAR SPECIES** The female is quite brown and the juvenile quite spotty, so could easily be mistaken for a Song or Mistle Thrush (p. 110). The male is quite similar to a Starling (p. 102) but has a much longer tail and different behaviour.

| JAN | FEB | MAR | APR | MAY | JUN | JUL | AUG | SEP | OCT | NOV | DEC |

SONG THRUSH

Turdus philomelos

Common woodland bird that thrives in suburbia.

Over most of the region this is the only 'spotty' thrush you are likely to see in a garden – certainly in gardens squashed together into the suburban patchwork. It is a shy bird that prefers to feed on the edge of a lawn or under shrubbery, places within reach of cover and safety. On the lawn it shares the Blackbird's (p. 106) fondness for worms and other invertebrates, and forages the same way, marching across the sward in stop-start fashion before the occasional lunge towards food. It is also the only garden bird that regularly smashes snail shells open by holding the molluscs in its bill and ramming them against a hard surface. Far smaller than a Blackbird, it is easily bullied by its relative. One of the great delights of the winter garden is to hear this bird's wonderful, wild song, often delivered during cold early mornings when it is barely light.

Considerably smaller than a Blackbird or Mistle Thrush (p. 110), the Song Thrush is not very much larger than a Starling (p. 102). It is well proportioned, with a relatively slim chest and medium-length tail. **ADULT** Attractive, with dark brown upperparts and very obvious spots on the paler breast and belly. The spots

well-proportioned

droplet-shaped spots

FACT FILE

FAMILY Turdidae (Thrushes). SIZE Length 20–22cm. FOOD Worms, snails and other invertebrates; also berries. SIMILAR SPECIES Redwing (p. 114), juvenile Blackbird and Mistle Thrush.

tend to be drop shaped, pointing upwards, rather than round (see Mistle Thrush), and the ground colour of the underside is less white than buff. **JUVENILE** Pale spots on mantle. **VOICE** Song a glorious accompaniment to winter dawn and dusk, and beyond. If you hear a bird song in pre-dawn darkness, it could be this bird's, with its studied repetition of each phrase, perfect enunciation and somewhat urgent feel. It has a large repertoire and

sings each phrase several times before moving on to the next, which is also repeated: 'hello, hello, hello, I'm a Song Thrush, I'm a Song Thrush, I'm a Song Thrush, It's cold, It's cold, It's cold, It's cold...' , and so on. Unique. Call is a gentle *tsip*, like an irritated person tutting. **MIGRATION** Resident in Britain, France and the Low Countries, but elsewhere birds migrate south, mainly to western and southern Europe.

 BREEDING March–July, 2–3 broods, and occasionally 4. **NEST** Well-shaped cup of grass, dead leaves, small twigs and moss, with an inner lining just of mud (unlike Blackbird). **EGGS** 3–6, incubated for 14–15 days. **YOUNG** Fledge at 12–16 days.

 Male Song Thrushes stop singing immediately after they have paired up, except for the dawn and evening chorus.

 The oldest known individual Song Thrush lived to 13 years.

MISTLE THRUSH

Turdus viscivorus

Locally common woodland bird, easily overlooked.

It might seem odd to say in a garden bird book, but you probably do not have this species in your garden. A good rule of thumb is to say that every suburban garden thrush is the smaller Song Thrush, p. 108). However, if you have a large garden with a big lawn without high fences, or live near playing fields, or have a tall tree nearby, the Mistle Thrush is well worth looking out for. In contrast to the cover-hugging Song Thrush, it has a habit of feeding right out in the open, for example in the middle of a large field. When it takes off, it does not make a burst for cover, but flies away with a heavy, up-and-down flight. Listen out for the irritable-sounding call, a loud, dry rattle. It is not normally sociable, but in late summer and autumn look for flocks made up of from one or more family parties, maybe comprising 8–20 birds.

This is quite a large bird, much larger than a Starling (p. 102), with an upright stance on the ground, a 'beer-gut' and a long tail. **ADULT** Has the spotty front of a thrush. Note that the spots are rounded, and they coalesce to make a smudge on either side of the middle of the breast. Key features not shared by Song Thrush: white spots at tip of tail, pale panel in wings and white under wing. **VOICE** Song (November–June) is neither as repetitive as a Song Thrush's, nor as languid as a Blackbird's (p. 106), with certain favourite phrases repeated, but at a greater pace than in a Blackbird's song. To many ears it is melancholic. It is often

relatively small head

upright posture

rounded spots on breast

heard in the afternoon and in windy weather, when other birds are silent. Call is an irritated rattle. **MIGRATION** Mainly resident in the west, but other populations migrate to southern Europe for the winter.

BREEDING March–June, two broods. **NEST** Cup nest of sticks, mixed with mud, often well above ground. **EGGS** 3–5, with female incubating for 15 days. **YOUNG** Leave nest after 14 days and are fed for another 14 days.

Male and female have virtually no display. It seems that the song is sufficient to bring the sexes together.

Mistle Thrushes get supremely aggressive in autumn. Some individuals and pairs commandeer a long-lasting berry tree, such as a Holly or, indeed, a Mistletoe, for their own use as a winter-berry store.

FACT FILE

FAMILY Turdidae (Thrushes). SIZE Length 26–29cm. FOOD Invertebrates and berries.
SIMILAR SPECIES Juvenile Blackbird and Song Thrush.

FIELDFARE

Turdus pilaris

Common bird of open woods; swaps north-east for south-west in winter.

In Britain, France and most of the Low Countries, the Fieldfare is very much a winter visitor. Ragged flocks, seen on the move in autumn, are an unmistakable sign of the changing seasons. In Scandinavia and Finland, by contrast, it is a summer bird, abundant in all kinds of scrubby areas, including gardens. When a winter visitor, it is more common in gardens in the late season, in the New Year, when the stocks of its favourite foods, wild berries, are beginning to run out. Then it is bolder and easier to see, even coming for apples and other fruits. This is an extremely sociable bird, almost always in flocks, which can number in the hundreds, either marching across fields, where the birds forage for invertebrates such as worms, or flying in famously uncoordinated groups. It also often nests in large, well-spaced colonies.

A large thrush, the Fieldfare is slightly bigger than a Blackbird

grey head and rump

velvet back

black tail

FACT FILE

FAMILY Turdidae (Thrushes). SIZE Length 24–28cm. FOOD Insects and worms, plus a lot of berries. SIMILAR SPECIES Song Thrush (p. 108), Mistle Thrush (p. 110) and Redwing (p. 114).

(p. 106), with a bold colour scheme. It hops across fields, and has a curious flight, looking flappy and inefficient, not very undulating. **ADULT** Very smart, with grey head and rump, black tail and velvet on back and wings; conventional thrush spots on breast. **VOICE** Song comprises ghastly discordant grating phrases strung together in long series. Call is a distinctive *shack* or *shack-shack*, often uttered by flying flocks. **MIGRATION** Resident in central parts of region, while northerly and eastern populations fly to western and southern Europe.

BREEDING May–July, 1–2 broods. Often colonial. **NEST** Bulky cup of grass and moss, lined with mud, which is then lined with grass; placed in fork of tree, or on stump or on the ground. **EGGS** 5–6, incubated for 11–14 days. **YOUNG** Fledge at 12–16 days.

The Fieldfare famously dive-bombs intruders to the nest and poos on them. Several nesting parents may take part, collectively pooing.

| JAN | FEB | MAR | APR | MAY | JUN | JUL | AUG | SEP | OCT | NOV | DEC |

REDWING

Turdus iliacus

Very common bird of northern scrub and open woodland; population evacuates north in winter.

This is the smallest of the thrushes, not much bigger than a Starling (p. 102). It is one of the two species, together with the Fieldfare (p. 112), that are nicknamed 'winter thrushes' in Britain and elsewhere, because flocks are a familiar sight in fields and gardens in the cold months of the year. It breeds abundantly in Iceland, Scandinavia and Finland. Redwings are easy to overlook due to their similarity to Song Thrushes (p. 108), and they also spend much time on the ground searching for worms and other food. In autumn they roam around in search of berries and, in common with Fieldfares, become more frequent visitors to gardens as 'wild' supplies begin to run out. The Redwing is extremely sociable, much more so than the Song Thrush, and may form flocks of hundreds. In early spring these flocks often make a delightful babbling sound as birds begin to sing in preparation for the breeding season.

Slightly smaller than a Song Thrush, the Redwing also has a slightly shorter tail, but is otherwise similar. Its flight is fast, and quite similar to that of a Starling. **ADULT** Easily and instantly told from a Song Thrush by its very prominent pale eyebrow, which gives its face a completely different look, as

pale eyebrow and moustache

russet flanks

though it has been applying make-up. The name Redwing refers to the underwing, although there is also a reddish wash on the flanks. **VOICE** Song a delightful short phrase with a slightly sighing air, going down the scale at first. Call is a sharp *tsee*, like a sharp intake of breath. Often heard overhead at night. **MIGRATION** Birds from Iceland, Scandinavia and the Baltic winter west and south, within Europe.

 BREEDING May–June, two broods. **NEST** A thick cup of grass, small twigs and moss, strengthened with mud, and placed in a tree, usually against a trunk; sometimes in sticks near the ground. **EGGS** 4–5, incubated for 11–15 days. **YOUNG** Fledge at 10–15 days.

 Tends not to spend each winter in the same place; in one season may winter in the UK, in the next in Greece.

FACT FILE

FAMILY Turdidae (Thrushes). SIZE Length 19–23cm. FOOD Worms and insects, and berries. SIMILAR SPECIES Song Thrush and other thrushes.

| JAN | FEB | MAR | APR | **MAY** | **JUN** | **JUL** | **AUG** | **SEP** | OCT | NOV | DEC |

SPOTTED FLYCATCHER

Muscicapa striata

Fairly common summer visitor to woods and gardens.

The Spotted Flycatcher is a rather featureless, small brown bird, yet it is easy to identify because of its eye-catching manner. One moment it will be perched upright, often on an elevated lookout post such as a dead branch, the next it launches into the air to catch a passing insect, then it lands again where it started, or nearby, immediately on the lookout for its next meal. When perched it looks restless, often flicking its tail, while in flight it swoops and flits with the expertise of a Swallow (p. 84), using its long wings. The Spotted Flycatcher is very much a summer bird, specializing in the fair-season glut of robust, juicy insects. It was once common and familiar in gardens, but is now much reduced in numbers. Gardens, with their heavy insect traffic and lots of open space, are the perfect habitat. The birds were famous for placing their nests on house walls, in creepers, on trellises and other places where they were easy to see.

An upright-perching, long-winged, large-headed small bird, its behaviour is very different from that of many brown birds. It is not

FACT FILE

FAMILY Muscicapidae (Flycatchers and Chats). SIZE Length 13.5–15cm. FOOD Various flying insects; a few small berries. SIMILAR SPECIES Robin (p. 120) and other small brown birds.

streaks on throat

upright stance

long wings

secretive at all, often perching in plain sight, and is quite tame. **ADULT** Mouse-brown above, pale on the underside, with some streaks on the throat (not spots) and crown. Dark eye in broad head. Pale edges to wing feathers. **YOUNG** Mildly pale spotted. **VOICE** Song is one of the truly terrible efforts of any small bird – a series of ghastly discordant squeaks. Typical call is a quiet *whiss-chuk*. **MIGRATION** Long-distance migrant to tropical Africa.

BREEDING May–August, two broods. **NEST** Often places nest on walls of buildings, or in creepers; also in trees against a trunk. Nest is a cup of grass, roots, plant down and feathers. **EGGS** 4–5, incubated for 11–15 days. **YOUNG** Fledge at 12–14 days, but may be fed for another three weeks out of the nest.

In contrast to many migrants, Spotted Flycatchers do not put on much extra fat before leaving. Instead they rely on getting enough food in transit, including in Saharan oases.

PIED FLYCATCHER

Ficedula hypoleuca

Locally common summer visitor to woodland areas.

It is a privileged garden that counts the Pied Flycatcher among its inhabitants, but in the northern parts of the region, including Scotland and Scandinavia, this smart bird quite readily shares our spaces, lured in by the provision of nest-boxes. So enamoured is this bird with artificial boxes, that where they are set up, it prefers them to natural tree-holes. The male often sings from the top of the box itself. Smaller than the Spotted Flycatcher (p. 116), the Pied nonetheless has a similar dependence on flying insects and has the same technique of setting off from a lookout perch to ambush them in mid-air. However, it does not return to the same perch as often after a sally, so moves around more, and is generally much more secretive. It is also a long-distance migrant to Europe, arriving in mid-April and leaving early, usually in August.

This species is smaller than the Spotted Flycatcher and more rotund, with a noticeably shorter tail. It repeatedly nervously cocks its tail.

smart black-and-white plumage

ADULT Instantly distinguishable from the Spotted Flycatcher by large white patch in wings, as well as white outer-tail feathers. It is a very smart bird, which always shows a sharp contrast between dark upperparts and almost milky-white, clean underparts.
MALE Smart black and white, with gleaming white underside, wing-panels and forehead.
FEMALE Dark brown above, slightly

dirty-white below and smaller white wing-panel.
VOICE Pleasing, slurred song-phrase; notes often go up and down. Call a sharp *pwit*. If you think you hear a Goldfinch (p. 146) in a wood, it might well be a Pied Flycatcher.
MIGRATION Long-distance migrant to West Africa, with a stopover in Spain and Portugal.

 BREEDING April–July, 1-2 broods.
NEST In a hole or nest-box; it is a loose cup of grass, leaves and other materials.
EGGS 5-7, incubated by female for 12-13 days.
YOUNG Fledge at 16-17 days.

★ Male may hold two territories, well separated, each with a different female apparently unaware of the other.

white spot on forehead varies

RIGHT: *FEMALE*

FAMILY Muscicapidae (Flycatchers and Chats). SIZE Length 12–13.5cm. FOOD Insects, both flying and non-flying. SIMILAR SPECIES Spotted Flycatcher.

JAN	FEB	MAR	APR	MAY	JUN	JUL	AUG	SEP	OCT	NOV	DEC

ROBIN

Erithacus rubecula

Often very common in woods and gardens.

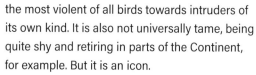

Once of the most instantly recognizable garden characters, the Robin is a great favourite of many. Few birds are so comfortable in the presence of humanity. This is the bird that accompanies gardeners in the course of their work, the one that sits on spades and often becomes tame enough to take food (especially mealworms) from the hand, or even enters a house. With its large eyes and rotund body, which it often ruffles in cold weather, as well as the signature orange-red breast, it invites our appreciation. It also has an endearing habit of singing virtually all year round, even in the middle of winter and in the dark – it is often assumed, wrongly, to be a Nightingale, a summer visitor. To cap it all, it often nests in gardens and may select unusual places, such as pockets of hung-up overcoats, watering cans and open drawers. It is not perfect, of course; it is one of

the most violent of all birds towards intruders of its own kind. It is also not universally tame, being quite shy and retiring in parts of the Continent, for example. But it is an icon.

In appearance the Robin is small but plump, with an upright stance. Usually instantly recognizable, it often curtseys when perched, or bobs its head and flicks its wings. Its flight is undulating, usually low down. **ADULT** Brown bird with orange-red breast, side of neck and forehead. It has large dark eyes. **JUVENILE** Familiar shape and actions, but quite different plumage – brown with pale spots, and some hint of orange on breast. **VOICE** Dominant year-round song, with a wistful air. Birds sing a phrase, pause, then sing another, pause and

FACT FILE

FAMILY Muscicapidae (Flycatchers and Chats). SIZE Length 12.5–14cm. FOOD Insects and various other invertebrates, especially worms; berries in autumn. SIMILAR SPECIES Dunnock (p. 130), other small brown birds and Black Redstart female (p. 122). In some continental gardens the Nightingale (*Luscinia megarhynchos*) may occur. It is larger and longer tailed than the Robin, without any orange, but the tail is rusty.

orange breast
and forehead
unmistakable

so on. The phrases may be long or short, and you can imagine them being answers to inaudible questions in an interview. The song is shrill, and often the phrases have fast/slow sequences. Call is a clean *tick*.
MIGRATION Mainly resident, but Scandinavian and Baltic birds move west and south within Europe in autumn.

BELOW: *JUVENILE*

 BREEDING March–June, two broods, occasionally three. **NEST** Often in a hollow in the ground or a tree cavity, or any number of artificial sites such as in an outbuilding or a greenhouse. Nest is a bulky cup of grass, dead leaves and moss. **EGGS** 2–6, incubated by female, fed by male for 12–15 days. **YOUNG** Fledge at 13–16 days.

Robins often feed in the shade and have large eyes. As a result, they see well in poor light and are often the first to sing during the dawn chorus.

Robins may 'get engaged' in midwinter, but do not formally breed until March or April.

BLACK REDSTART

Phoenicurus ochruros

A town and village bird in parts of the Continent; localized.

In a few parts of the region, such as France, Germany and the Low Countries, this is a common and familiar garden bird, although it is rare elsewhere, including in Britain. It has a curious attraction to buildings, seeing them as little more than extensions of the rocky habitats – cliffs, crags and mountain slopes – that are its natural home. It is very much a bird of rooftops, and commonly sings from high perches, including aerials, the top floors of buildings, and even industrial sites such as warehouses and cranes, while it nests in holes in frayed brickwork, piles of rubble, outhouses or on the ground. It prefers to stand upright and hop on the ground, rarely perching in a tree or shrub, but content with wires and rocks. In common with the Redstart (p. 124), it has the strange habit of shivering its tail constantly, for reasons that nobody has yet fathomed.

BELOW: *MALE*

dark plumage

orange tail

A songbird with dark plumage, the Black Redstart is usually seen around buildings, including industrial sites. **ADULT** Orange tail, flitting flight and dark plumage are giveaways. **MALE** Unique sooty-black with a prominent white wing-bar, to go with the orange tail. **FEMALE** Unique sooty-brown all over (including a dark throat, see Redstart), to go with the orange tail. **JUVENILE** Similar to female.

VOICE Song is unique and strange. It is in two parts: first an introductory trill, then a very odd-sounding dry rattle like ball-bearings rubbing together. Call is a sharp *weet*. **MIGRATION** Complicated: a summer visitor (March–October) to its continental range, wintering further south around the Mediterranean. Some birds winter in Britain instead.

ABOVE AND LEFT:
FEMALE

 BREEDING April–July, two broods, occasionally three. **NEST** Placed in a hole or crevice in a building or rock. It is an unimaginative cup of dry grass, moss, animal wool and hair. **EGGS** 4–6, incubated for 12–16 days. **YOUNG** Fledge at 12–19 days.

 Nests have been found on building ledges 45m above the ground – a bit hairy for fledging young.

 A male may sing 5,000 times a day.

F A C T   F I L E

FAMILY Muscicapidae (Flycatchers and Chats). **SIZE** Length 13–14.5cm. **FOOD** Mainly insects, with some spiders and a few berries in autumn. **SIMILAR SPECIES** Redstart, Robin (p. 120) and other small brown birds.

| JAN | FEB | MAR | **APR** | **MAY** | **JUN** | **JUL** | **AUG** | **SEP** | OCT | NOV | DEC |

REDSTART

Phoenicurus phoenicurus

Locally common in woodland edges and scrub.

A common and familiar garden bird over much of continental Europe, the Redstart is much scarcer in Britain, and mainly found in the west and north. It readily takes to nest-boxes, though, throughout its range. Closely related to the Robin (p. 120), it catches its food in similar ways. Most typically, it drops down from a slightly elevated perch on to the ground, catching insects it has spotted; it also hops on the ground. However, it additionally feeds among the leaves of trees or shrubs, where it can be difficult to spot. Both this species and the Black Redstart (p. 122) have conspicuous orange tails that they constantly shiver – this is by far the easiest way to identify them. In contrast to its relative, the Redstart is a long-distance migrant, wintering in tropical Africa. Its delightful, slightly apologetic song is commonly heard from April onwards, and it departs Europe mainly during September.

A small, slender, restless bird, the Redstart's tail-quiver is a giveaway. It has large eyes and strong legs. **ADULT** Both sexes have an orange tail. **MALE** Very handsome, with an orange-red breast, grey back,

FACT FILE

FAMILY Muscicapidae (Flycatchers and Chats). SIZE Length 13–14.5cm. FOOD Insects and other invertebrates, including worms; a few berries. SIMILAR SPECIES Black Redstart, Robin and other small brown birds.

white forehead

black face
and throat

orange
breast

black face-mask and conspicuous white forehead. **FEMALE** Similar to
the Black Redstart, but with warmer, browner tones to the plumage,
especially below, and a whitish throat. **VOICE** Song easy to recognize
when you realize the format. Like the Black Redstart's song, it is in
two parts. The first is a gentle, slightly sighing *hey diddle-diddle*,
always much the same. The second part is very different and varies
enormously from phrase to phrase; it can comprise imitations of other
birds, or be something original. It gives a gentle *wheet* call – a sound
similar to that of many other birds – but it is often combined with *tuk*
notes to give *wheet, tuk, tuk*, which is characteristic. **MIGRATION** Long-
distance migrant to Africa just south of the Sahara.

BREEDING April–July, two broods. **NEST** In a crevice in a tree
or stump, or in a building; often uses nest-boxes. Nest is a
loose cup of grass, moss and other soft materials, lined with feathers.
EGGS 5–7, incubated for 11–14 days. Young leave nest at 16–17 days.

The male Redstart sometimes sings from inside the nest-hole,
with just its white forehead showing.

HOUSE SPARROW

Passer domesticus

Abundant anywhere there are people, from villages to cities.

It is good to have neighbours that appreciate us and, in the case of the House Sparrow, which need us. Around the world, the House Sparrow only occurs near the dwellings and activities of people, including by farms and arable fields. It is a restless companion, always doing something, from dust-bathing in earth to indulging in skirmishes, which often have a loud, chirping audience participation, as if a crowd were egging on the protagonists. This bird is intensely sociable, living in long-term, stable groups in the same neighbourhood – sometimes individual sparrows stay longer in a housing estate than people. It can be provided with any kind of seed, on a hanging feeder or table, and also takes various scraps.

The House Sparrow is the archetypal small brown bird, although it is quite robust compared to many. The label is harsh on the handsome male, too. However, all others are measured by this abundant species. Note the lack of any obvious streaks or spots on the underside, which is important. It is also famously dishevelled and grimy looking. **MALE** Grey cap and cheek, without a cheek-spot (see Tree Sparrow, p. 128).

BELOW: *MALE (NOTE NO WHITE ON TAIL)*

grey crown and grey cheeks

Black on throat and breast is variable. Black bill in summer. In winter, male's head and throat markings are less smart and distinct. Bill is paler. **FEMALE** More distinctive than it looks – for one thing, there are no obvious streaks at all on the breast or belly, which is unusual. For another, it has a distinctive pale eyebrow. **VOICE** Unusually, it has no obvious song. It just gives various cheeps and chirps that vary according to its mood. A series of emphatic cheeps is the best attempt at territorial proclamation. **MIGRATION** Nothing much. In rural areas it sometimes moves a short distance in late summer, almost as if going on a holiday.

Pale eyebrow

ABOVE: *FEMALE*
BELOW: *MALE*

![bird icon] **BREEDING** April–August, usually two broods, but sometimes three or even four. **NEST** Straw stuffed into a box, gutter or crevice to make a rough dome with a side entrance; also sometimes in a dense bush. Often occupies nest-boxes intended for other birds, such as House Martins. **EGGS** 4–5, incubated for two weeks. **YOUNG** Remain in nest for another 15–17 days, fed by both parents on insects.

![star icon] The amount of black on a male's throat/breast-patch is directly related to its fighting ability – the more it has, the more accomplished it is.

FACT FILE

FAMILY Passeridae (Sparrows). SIZE Length 14–16cm. FOOD Various seeds and scraps.
SIMILAR SPECIES Tree Sparrow, Greenfinch (female, p. 145) and Reed Bunting (p. 156).

| JAN | FEB | MAR | APR | MAY | JUN | JUL | AUG | SEP | OCT | NOV | DEC |

TREE SPARROW

Passer montanus

Locally common in both villages and rural areas.

The Tree Sparrow is slightly smaller and invariably better presented than its scruffy counterpart, the House Sparrow (p. 126), rarely looking anything other than immaculate. On the whole it tends to shun the urban parks, grimy buildings, alleyways and small gardens frequented by its colleague, and instead is more of a countryside bird, found in farmland, small villages and parks with old trees; it usually nests in holes in trees. Where it occurs, however, it is just as common in gardens as the House Sparrow and uses feeding stations with the same enthusiasm. It also readily takes to nest-boxes, and these can be important for the conservation of the species. In Britain and other parts of the region, it has been suffering from a long-term decline. Tree Sparrows are very sociable, and will join flocks of other seed-eating birds, including House Sparrows. In these flocks you might notice something unusual. Male and female House Sparrows look quite different, but male and female Tree Sparrows are alike.

This bird looks like a small sparrow dolled up for an evening out, smart and well scrubbed (or a sparrow sticking to a New Year's resolution – slimmer, prettier, tidier, and so on). **ADULT** Caramel-brown cap, neat white cheeks and collar, and black cheek-spot (all different

BELOW: MIXED FLOCK WITH HOUSE SPARROWS

FACT FILE

FAMILY Passeridae (Sparrows). SIZE Length 12–14cm. FOOD Grain and seeds, with insects in the breeding season. SIMILAR SPECIES House Sparrow and Reed Bunting (male, p. 156)

chestnut cap

black spot on cheek

from the House Sparrow). **JUVENILE** Looks exactly like a juvenile
Tree Sparrow should look – a washed-out version of the adult. **VOICE**
No obvious song. Similar cheep to House Sparrow, but definitely two
syllables and slightly higher pitched. It also has a flight call, a harsh *tek*.
MIGRATION Mainly resident.

BREEDING April–July, 2–3 broods.
NEST Made from grass and twigs
stuffed unashamedly into a cavity, to make
a dome; uses tree-holes and holes in walls.
EGGS 5–6, incubated for 11–14 days. **YOUNG**
Fledge at 12–14 days.

Oddly, the Tree Sparrow takes over
the House Sparrow's mantle as the
urban sprog in many huge Asian cities.

DUNNOCK

Prunella modularis

Common but easily overlooked in scrubby and bushy areas.

One of the most intriguing birds in the garden, the Dunnock is so self-effacing that it barely registers in the consciousness. It seemingly does everything to keep under the radar. Almost literally – it feeds on the ground by creeping, seemingly barefooted, around the shrubbery, rarely landing on a bird table and certainly never on hanging feeders. It moves furtively, with its very own shuffling gait, nervously flicking its wings and tail. Its plumage is sober and dull, with nothing more exciting than dark streaks. The song, although tuneful, also manages to be less vehement than a Wren's (p. 96) and less beautiful than a Robin's (p. 120) – it has been described as a flat warble.

red eye

greyish head

thin bill

sparrow-like wing pattern

Yet the Dunnock is a common and successful species, and its life is full of surprises. Any bird that is given to pairing up with multiple mates, bodily rejecting the sperm of an unpreferred male and forming titanic clashes between rival males, is well worth more attention than it gets.

The Dunnock is the quintessential small brown bird but note how thin the bill is. It indicates an insectivorous diet, in contrast to sparrows and other streaky birds, which are seed eaters. **ADULT** Rich brown, heavily streaked above and below; pink legs and red eyes. Note the obvious grey on the head and breast. No other small streaky birds has this. **JUVENILE** Has more streaks than adult, and the grey is barely visible. **VOICE** Song is a sweet, cyclical warble, sounding like the squeaky wheels of a trolley. Every song phrase sounds the same (a pattern similar to the Wren's song, but quite different from the variety of the Robin's song). Almost everyone with a garden will have heard this common song. Call is a very common garden sound, a loud *seep* with a slightly strained, broken tone. **MIGRATION** Mainly resident, but Scandinavian and Baltic birds migrate to southern and western Europe for the winter.

 BREEDING April–July, two broods, occasionally three. **NEST** Placed well hidden in a tree, shrub or rank vegetation, well above ground. It is a sturdy cup of twigs, leaves and moss, lined with fine materials, built by the female. **EGGS** 4–5, bright blue, incubated for 12–13 days. **YOUNG** In nest fed by female and any male that has copulated with her (could be several males). They fledge at 11–12 days but are fed for two weeks afterwards.

★ Famous for its complicated breeding arrangements, in which there may be monogamy, polyandry (female with several males), polygyny (male with several females) or a combination of the latter.

★ Copulation in the Dunnock takes just a quarter of a second.

★ Alpha and beta males compete for females, but the females want all the attention, so they will literally hide behind bushes and mate with a beta male when an alpha male's back is turned.

F A C T   F I L E

FAMILY Prunellidae (Accentors). **SIZE** Length 13–14.5cm. **FOOD** Small insects; a few berries and seeds. **SIMILAR SPECIES** House Sparrow (p. 126) and Robin.

| JAN | FEB | MAR | APR | MAY | JUN | JUL | AUG | SEP | OCT | NOV | DEC |

MEADOW PIPIT

Anthus pratensis

Abundant in open country, mainly in the north.

Not many garden enthusiasts are familiar with the Meadow Pipit, although it is abundant in parts of Iceland, Scandinavia and northern Britain. It could, however, touch down in large rural gardens with an open aspect, and it certainly flies over millions of gardens in autumn and spring, largely undetected. An open country bird, it bears a faint resemblance to a miniature thrush, with its streaky breast and brown plumage, but it is only the size of a Great Tit (p. 70). Pipits do not hop, but instead walk or run across the ground. Outside the breeding season they are extremely sociable, and are usually met with in flocks. Although they are not long-distance migrants, Meadow Pipits often evacuate higher ground in autumn, or simply move away from breeding areas, including most of Scandinavia. This is when you might see or hear a flock flying overhead, usually early in the morning.

The Meadow Pipit is a slim, streamlined bird that walks along the ground with a horizontal posture. It often runs and will wag its tail. It can easily be mistaken for a wagtail but the tail is shorter. The flight is very weak and undulating. It has a curious habit of being hesitant when

often resembles miniature thrush

FACT FILE

FAMILY Motacillidae (Pipits and Wagtails). SIZE Length 14–15.5cm. FOOD Mainly invertebrates, small seeds. SIMILAR SPECIES Sparrows, Reed Bunting (p. 156), thrushes and Dunnock (p. 130).

slim body, very
streaked

walks on
the ground

landing, seemingly changing its mind multiple times before settling.
Given a close look, it has a very long hind-claw, typical of a bird that is
on the ground a lot. **ADULT** 'Miniature thrush' with heavy streaks above
and below on dull buff plumage; blank expression, pink legs, pale
wing-bars. White outer-tail feathers. **VOICE** Song is unlikely to be heard
in a garden. Call is *sip-sip* or *sip-sip-sip* – faintly like the sound made
by flicking your finger softly on a raincoat. **MIGRATION** Complicated.
Northern (Scandinavian and Icelandic) populations fly south to Britain
and the Continent, but many other populations also make modest local
movements.

BREEDING March–August, two broods. **NEST** Cup of dry
grasses and a little moss, placed on the ground carefully
under cover of, for example, heather. **EGGS** 3–5, sometimes more,
incubated for 11–15 days, quicker than many birds. **YOUNG** Leave nest
before they can fly properly, at 14–15 days.

The Meadow Pipit has a great display, launching into the air
while singing, then spiralling back down on static wings, tail
up – like a paper aeroplane.

JAN	FEB	MAR	APR	MAY	JUN	JUL	AUG	SEP	OCT	NOV	DEC

PIED & WHITE WAGTAILS

Motacilla alba

Very common in towns, cities, farms and fields.

The Pied Wagtail (White Wagtail on the Continent) is not so much a garden bird as a neighbourhood bird. It does touch down in gardens, but it is more typical of parks, playing fields, roadsides and – oddly enough – car parks and roofs. It is also very common where livestock is farmed. It is a distinctive bird, with a remarkably long tail that it does indeed wag incessantly. On the ground it alternates a stately walk with quick bursts of running, as if it is on a high-intensity interval training regime. It is certainly restless and energetic, and often leaps into the air after a flying insect. Its flight is bounding, and a long-tailed bird following steep undulations is likely to be a wagtail. Some wagtails are solitary, while others are sociable in winter, forming flocks on waterlogged fields, sewage farms and other areas with plenty of invertebrates. On winter nights Pied Wagtails often roost in large groups.

The walking gait and long tail is very distinctive, although the Magpie's (p. 56) is the same. The flight is bounding, often low down, and is also notable. **ADULT** Black-and-white plumage, often with plenty

BELOW: *MALE SUMMER*

black-and-white plumage

black legs

long tail

LEFT: *IMMATURE WINTER*

BELOW: *MALE*

of grey. It always has a white head, unlike other garden birds; also white wing-bars. British (Pied) Wagtail: black and white with dark back. Continental (White) Wagtail: very smart, pale grey back. Pied male has a black back; female a dark grey back. White male has a sharp border between the black cap and a grey back (not in female). **JUVENILE** Complicated – look for overall shape. May even have yellow on face. **VOICE** Song is a medley of calls. Makes an easily recognized, somewhat slurred *tschi-zik* call in flight. **MIGRATION** Resident in some places (Britain, much of France, the Low Countries, Germany), but the rest are migrants that winter as far south as Africa.

 BREEDING April–August, two broods. **NEST** Placed in a cavity of almost any kind, from a hole in a building to a bank, a pipe, the thatch of a roof, and so on. It is a cup of twigs, roots, moss and leaves. **EGGS** 5–6, incubated for 12–14 days by both sexes. **YOUNG** Fledge at 13–16 days, already wagging their tails.

★ No one definitively knows why the birds wag their tails incessantly.

★ Pied Wagtails sometimes roost communally on municipal Christmas trees, presumably benefiting from the weak warmth of fairy lights.

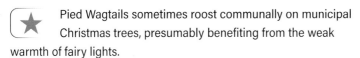

FACT FILE

FAMILY Motacillidae (Pipits and Wagtails). SIZE Length 16.5–19cm. FOOD Various insects.
SIMILAR SPECIES Grey Wagtail (p. 136) and perhaps Long-tailed Tit (p. 66).

| JAN | FEB | MAR | APR | MAY | JUN | JUL | AUG | SEP | OCT | NOV | DEC |

GREY WAGTAIL

Motacilla cinerea

Locally common by rivers; in winter by still water, including ponds.

The Grey Wagtail is even slimmer and longer tailed than the Pied Wagtail (p. 134), although it is the lemon-yellow underparts, especially under the tail, that most readily identify it. It is also much more closely associated with water than the Pied Wagtail – a super-streamlined bird that lines up along streams, including fast torrents and mere trickles. Unless your garden incorporates a riverside, you will only get a visit in winter, when the Grey Wagtail expands its range to include ponds and even puddles. If your pond includes a small waterfall, that is Grey Wagtail heaven, and a big attractant. This bird is much less sociable than the Pied Wagtail, never occurring in flocks, just family parties in the late summer. If anything, its tail wagging is even more exaggerated than that of the Pied Wagtail – indeed, the whole rear end goes up and down.

This is a slim, lanky and slightly bottom-heavy wagtail. **ADULT** Always neat, it is smoky-grey on the mantle, wings and head, and

grey back

lemon yellow, especially at rear

pink legs

FACT FILE

FAMILY Motacillidae (Pipits and Wagtails). SIZE Length 17–20cm. FOOD Mostly invertebrates, but sometimes eats tadpoles. SIMILAR SPECIES Pied Wagtail and Yellow Wagtail (*Moticilla flava*).

ABOVE: *FEMALE*

variably lemon-yellow on the underparts. Note that the legs are pink (those of the Pied Wagtail are black). **MALE** Throat as black as ink, making sharp contrast with the white moustache-stripe. Black less clean in winter. **FEMALE** Whitish, sometimes with some black stubble. **VOICE** Song seldom heard in gardens. Call is a sharply enunciated *zi-zit*. The Grey Wagtail is the 'well-bred' wagtail, with perfect diction. **MIGRATION** Some birds are resident, while others move relatively modest distances away from uplands or frozen areas.

 BREEDING March–August, 1–2 broods. **NEST** Placed in a hole or hollow by the water, especially on a bridge or by a weir or waterfall. It is a cup of various grasses, twigs, moss and leaves. **EGGS** 4–6, incubated for 11–14 days. **YOUNG** Leave nest at 11–13 days.

BELOW: *MALE*

Grey Wagtails are aggressive in defence of their territory. It has been known for a bird to hold another's head under the water and drown it.

| JAN | FEB | MAR | APR | MAY | JUN | JUL | AUG | SEP | OCT | NOV | DEC |

BULLFINCH

Pyrrhula pyrrhula

Fairly common but shy bird of woods and scrub.

Looking like a Chaffinch (p. 140) that has just visited a tailor, the Bullfinch is invariably immaculately presented – and its stunningly bright, contrasting plumage ensures that it is one of the garden's most striking birds. Even the youngsters, which lack the black cap, still manage to convey an ineffable neatness. Despite its brilliance, though, the Bullfinch is quiet, shy and self-effacing. It is very easy to overlook, often feeding quietly on the buds of fruit trees or forsythia up in the topmost branches. It can even be overlooked when it comes to hanging feeders, as it often does, since it comes without ceremony – no loud calls, no bickering, no fuss. It is mainly a bird of quieter gardens, often with woodland nearby, and it also likes hedgerows and scrub. It is present all year and sometimes builds its nest in garden bushes – furtively of course. Its fondness for buds can get it into trouble with commercial fruit growers and gardeners.

This is a plump finch with a broad head; the thick bill forms an even curve with the head. It has a relatively powerful, undulating flight. Very shy, it is extremely easy to flush, which can be maddening. **ADULT** The black cap is the best way to distinguish it from the Chaffinch, rather than having to judge the colour of the breast, which can look very bright pink on the latter bird. Note the black wings and tail and – crucially – the white rump, a very important identifying feature. **MALE** Stunning pink-red breast, the colour of a strawberry smoothie, and ashy-grey back. **FEMALE** Plum-coloured breast and grey-brown back. **JUVENILE** No black cap. Always in company with adults. **VOICE** Song hardly ever heard – a creaky phrase sounding faintly like a pub sign creaking in the wind. Call is a gentle, somewhat downbeat *puu* with variations – but the Bullfinch

BELOW: *FEMALE (LEFT), MALE (RIGHT)*

heavy-headed

black cap
and bill

stunning,
bold colours

is a notably quiet bird, in contrast to most other finches.
MIGRATION Mainly resident.

ABOVE: *MALE*
BELOW: *FEMALE*

BREEDING April–July, 1–3 broods. **NEST**
Ramshackle pile of twigs, moss and lichen but
with a very neat cup within, placed in a bush 1–2m above
ground. **EGGS** 4–5, incubated for 12–14 days. **YOUNG**
Leave nest at 14–16 days.

In spring, Bullfinches develop small pouches
on either side of the floor of the mouth to help
them carry food to the young – a cubic centimetre of
extra capacity.

Bullfinches have often been kept in captivity
and taught to whistle human tunes – including
the German national anthem.

FACT FILE

FAMILY Fringillidae (Finches). SIZE Length 15.5–17cm. FOOD Seeds, buds and shoots.
SIMILAR SPECIES Chaffinch.

| JAN | FEB | MAR | APR | MAY | JUN | JUL | AUG | SEP | OCT | NOV | DEC |

CHAFFINCH

Fringilla coelebs

Abundant in woods, farmland and towns.

No less than one of Europe's most common birds, the Chaffinch is a woodland bird made good. Although it avoids the densest of urban areas, anywhere in suburbia, rural villages or neighbourhoods with extensive tree cover, it will thrive. In spring, gardens resound to the Chaffinch's simple but cheerful song; in winter, if you leave seed on the ground or on a tray-feeder, flocks will gather, every so often flushing and showing off their white wing-bars as they flee. The Chaffinch is unusual among finches for switching its diet completely from seeds in winter to insects in spring and summer; most other finches take only minimal insects. The Chaffinch often nests in bushes and shrubs in gardens and, in common with its relatives, is a master builder, constructing a very neat and tasteful cup, using multiple materials. Few garden projects are so perfect.

complex white wing-bar

white shoulder-patch (here partially covered

pink breast

long tail

FACT FILE

FAMILY Fringillidae (Finches). SIZE Length 14–16cm. FOOD Seeds in autumn and winter, insects in summer. SIMILAR SPECIES Brambling (p. 142), House Sparrow (p. 126), Greenfinch (females, p. 145) and Hawfinch. The Hawfinch (*Coccothraustes coccothraustes*) comes to continental European gardens. It is larger, with a massive bill and head, and short tail, with a different wing pattern.

In appearance, this is a very slim songbird with a relatively long tail, which at times appears awkwardly glued on. Very adaptable, it feeds on the ground and up in the trees and can even perform sallies to catch insects in flight. Otherwise, its flight is strong and undulating. When perched it often adopts a horizontal posture; other finches sit upright. **ADULT** Distinctive for its complex wing-pattern, and the identification clincher is the white shoulders, in both sexes. It has white outer-tail feathers and the rump is grey-green. **MALE** Colourful in spring, with bluish-grey head, pink breast and brown back. Faded colours in autumn and winter. **FEMALE** Lacks bright colours – just brown and buff. **VOICE** Song is a cheerful, rattling phrase, which accelerates and ends with a flourish. It is a dominant sound in less urban gardens and spaces in February–June. Best-known call is a very cheerful *pink-pink*. **MIGRATION** Resident except for Baltic and Scandinavian breeding birds, which migrate south and west within continental Europe in autumn.

ABOVE: *MALE*

ABOVE LEFT: *FEMALE*

BREEDING March–July, usually one brood. **NEST** Very neat, deep cup of moss bound with cobwebs, with lichen and bark on the outside; it is placed in a fork in a tree or shrub, fairly high up (35m recorded). **EGGS** 4–5, incubated for 10–16 days. **YOUNG** Fed on insects and leave nest at 13–16 days.

Young male Chaffinches learn their songs from their fathers and other males in the neighbourhood. This local learning leads to the formation of distinctive dialects.

Recent research has shown that individual Chaffinches have distinct personalities. For example, some are consistently bolder and more inquisitive than their more circumspect colleagues.

| JAN | FEB | MAR | APR | MAY | JUN | JUL | AUG | SEP | OCT | NOV | DEC |

BRAMBLING

Fringilla montifringilla

Abundant in scrubby areas in north; much more localized woodland bird in winter.

The Brambling is the northern equivalent of the Chaffinch (p. 140), a truly abundant bird of Norway, Sweden and Finland, occurring right up to the Arctic Circle, breeding in woodland and scrub. In winter it reverts to a different lifestyle, coming south in search of just one thing: the seeds of beech trees (mast). Later in the winter, usually after Christmas, it also comes into gardens, joining flocks of Chaffinches at seed trays, on the ground or at hanging feeders. The two species are closely related, and it is surprising how similar they look, despite the Brambling's very obvious orange wash (which perfectly matches the colour of fallen beech leaves). The Brambling is shyer than the Chaffinch, flying off at the slightest disturbance.

LEFT: *MALE LATE WINTER*

yellow bill

orange shoulder-patch

orange chest

spots on flanks

BELOW: *FEMALE*

ABOVE: *FEMALE (NOTE GREY COLLAR)*

This species is slightly portlier than the Chaffinch, with a shorter tail. **ADULT** Always distinguished from the similar Chaffinch by orange-apricot wash to plumage, subtle or obvious. Also has a black tail and white rump. Another feature is the rash of spots on the flanks. **MALE** From February very smart with black head and back, often looking mottled at other times. Bill yellow. **FEMALE** Orange-washed version of Chaffinch female. **VOICE** Song is a flat buzz, like a depressed Greenfinch's. Call is a 'parrot-like' twanging note. **MIGRATION** Summer visitor to Fenno-Scandia, the birds retreating in autumn over temperate Europe and the Mediterranean.

BREEDING May–June, 1–2 broods. **NEST** Large but very neat cup of moss, grass, cobwebs, feathers and bark, placed in a tree (usually a conifer), well above ground. **EGGS** 5–7, incubated for 11–12 days. **YOUNG** Fledge at 11–13 days.

Breeding further north, the Brambling's nest is larger than that of its relative, the Chaffinch, and has more feathers in its lining.

FACT FILE

FAMILY Fringillidae (Finches). SIZE Length 14–16cm. FOOD Seeds (especially beech) in autumn and winter, insects in summer. SIMILAR SPECIES Chaffinch.

JAN	FEB	MAR	APR	MAY	JUN	JUL	AUG	SEP	OCT	NOV	DEC

GREENFINCH

Chloris chloris

Very common in gardens and scrubby habitats.

Many people notice the Greenfinch for its aggression at birdfeeders, and its habit of monopolizing perches. When a pair of Greenfinches arrives at a hanging feeder, the birds sit on either side, munching away, unable to be dislodged by any smaller birds. The seed husks fall from their bills as they feast. Suburbia suits the Greenfinch, providing a fantastic range of plants, including flowers, for its broad taste in seeds. One moment it will be feeding from sunflowers on the flowerheads, the next it will be on the ground, taking seeds from a stray dandelion trumpet. Studies have shown that it utilizes more than 200 species of plant. It is a highly sociable bird, gathering in flocks in winter, and pairs tend to nest close by other pairs, constituting a small summer party known as a neighbourhood group. Greenfinches are also noisy, often singing and calling from the tops of trees and shrubs, Leylandii cypresses being a favourite. In spring and summer, males perform a song flight, describing a circle or figure of eight at treetop height.

BELOW: *MALE*

gorgeous apple-green

thick pink bill

yellow bar along wing

FACT FILE

FAMILY Fringillidae (Finches). SIZE Length 14–16cm. FOOD Unrivalled range of seeds; also a few insects. SIMILAR SPECIES House Sparrow (female, p. 127) and Siskin (p. 148).

This is a tubby finch with a noticeably short tail and, when perched, an upright stance (see Chaffinch, p. 140). The bill is large and very thick, and it makes a good weapon at birdfeeders. The Greenfinch carries a permanent frowning expression. **ADULT** Ranges from bright apple-green to greenish-brown, with a bright yellow wing-bar along

ABOVE: *FEMALE*

the wing edge. The bill is pink. **MALE** Brighter green than female, and has a pinker bill and large wing-bar. **FEMALE** Less bright green, with smaller wing-bar. **JUVENILE** Streakier, especially below (still has yellow wing-bar). **VOICE** Song is a series of dry trills, each on a different pitch, punctuated by intermittent, emphatic drawn-out wheezes. It is heard from March and right through the summer. Call is a simple *chip-chip*, heard especially in flight. **MIGRATION** Mainly resident, but northern populations move southwards to milder climates in Europe.

 BREEDING April–August, two broods. **NEST** Bulky cup of grasses and moss, placed in a tree or tall bush, often against the trunk. **EGGS** 4–5, incubated for 12–14 days. **YOUNG** Fed on regurgitated seed paste. They fledge at 13–16 days.

Unpaired male Greenfinches sometimes help a pair to feed their young at the nest. They seem to do this to curry favour with a potential mate for next year.

The Greenfinch is able to eat ultra-poisonous yew seeds.

| JAN | FEB | MAR | APR | MAY | JUN | JUL | AUG | SEP | OCT | NOV | DEC |

GOLDFINCH

Carduelis carduelis

Very common in weedy areas, gardens and scrub.

The Goldfinch adds colour and effervescence to the dullest of days. It has everything going for it: gorgeous to look at, interesting to observe, making attractive sounds and being both common and easy to identify. It is typical for this species to visit gardens in flocks, the members often monopolizing hanging birdfeeders for a short while, constantly conversing with each other in a fluent twitter. Individuals are often belligerent with each other. Although present all year this is an abundant summer bird due to its habit of late breeding. Members of flocks often perch upright on treetops and sing. This species also has the interesting habit of feeding on seeds from herbs, balancing on the heads with a flit of golden

distinctive black, white and red head

white spots on wings and tail.

wings. All over, flocks of Goldfinches could be described as the flitterati twitterati glitterati.

Small, about the size of a Blue Tit (p. 68), the Goldfinch typically perches with an upright posture. It flies with rapid, fluent wingbeats. The red, white and black head, allied to the ivory-coloured bill and toffee-coloured breast, make it unique. **JUVENILE** Lacks the colourful head, the dark eye giving it a forlorn expression. **VOICE** Song is a medley of liquid notes, with unexpectedly harsh chatters thrown in. Call is an easily recognized *tickle-it*. **MIGRATION** Present all year, but many individuals migrate south for a short distance in winter (for example from Britain to France).

 BREEDING May–August, usually two broods, but sometimes three (young can be seen well into September). **NEST** Gloriously neat cup of moss and other plant material, lined with copious plant down, often from thistles. It is often placed at the very end of a branch. **EGGS** 4–6, incubated for two weeks. **YOUNG** Remain in nest for another two weeks.

 The male's bill is 1mm (10 per cent) longer than the female's, making it better at extracting seeds from teasel heads.

FACT FILE

FAMILY Fringillidae (Finches). SIZE Length 12–13.5cm. FOOD Seeds, especially those of thistles, but also dandelions, lavender and teasels. A few insects in summer. SIMILAR SPECIES None.

| JAN | FEB | MAR | APR | MAY | JUN | JUL | AUG | SEP | OCT | NOV | DEC |

SISKIN

Spinus spinus

Fairly common in conifer woods and streamside alders; gardens in winter.

A shy forest bird, the Siskin is in some ways an accidental garden stray. However, the lure of a good seed or nut food source is too much for it to resist, and it can become a regular where hanging feeders are provided, especially those that are not far away from coniferous woods and plantations. When first encountered, the Siskin can be mistaken for a small ('baby') Greenfinch (p. 144), having the same yellow wing-bars and overall green plumage. However, it is far streakier, has a much smaller bill and, intriguingly, has an ingrained habit of frequently feeding upside down, something it does when feeding on cones in the treetops. It is most strongly associated with spruce trees, where it usually breeds, but in winter it can also be found on larches, birches and, in particular, alders. Even a single tree may attract a small flock feeding quietly up in the topmost branches. Due to its dry diet it drinks frequently.

This small, Blue Tit-sized (p. 68) finch tends to be seen in treetops, feeding acrobatically. The bill is sharply pointed and the tail notched.

BELOW: *MALE*

BELOW RIGHT: *FEMALE*

FACT FILE

FAMILY Fringillidae (Finches). SIZE Length 11–12.5cm. FOOD Seeds, usually taken in trees, or on the ground if fallen. Minimal number of insects in breeding season. SIMILAR SPECIES Greenfinch and Serin (p. 150).

coal black
cap

yellow-green
wing-bars

streaks on
flanks

ADULT When at rest, the yellow wing-bars go across the wings, rather than along the edge of the wing, as in the Greenfinch. In contrast to the Greenfinch, the flanks are heavily streaked. **MALE** Smart, with coal-black crown and chin, and lime-green back without many streaks. **FEMALE** Lacks black markings (including black chin, unlike female Redpoll, p. 152), and is streakier on back. **JUVENILE** Paler than similar female. **VOICE** Song is force of nature, a quiet, fizzing, demented babbling, often interspersed with squeaky calls and strange buzzes that sound like bursts of flatulence. Call is a slightly pathetic ('sissy') *dwee*, with a questioning air, rising in pitch. **MIGRATION** Variable numbers of birds move south after breeding, some moving considerable distances, but the species is present all year in much of the region.

BREEDING April–July, squeezing in two broods. Does not normally nest in gardens. **NEST** Typically neat finch effort, a cup of various plant materials such as small twigs, grass and moss, with some cobwebs. **EGGS** 3–5, incubated for 11–14 days by female. **YOUNG** Fed mainly on crushed seeds and leave nest at 13–15 days.

The muscles for opening the bill are just as strong as the muscles for biting, so Siskins insert the bill into tight spaces between scales on spruce cones and prise them open.

SERIN

Serinus serinus

Locally common garden and village bird; likes the sun.

A common continental European garden bird mysteriously absent from Britain, the Serin is a pocket dynamo, its speed dial set to maximum. It must sleep well at night. It has a habit of perching on the tops of trees, especially cypresses, singing with all its might, but soon gets bored, at which it might swap perches or indulge in a delightful song flight, in which it flies up to a height, then glides slowly down on curiously slow wingbeats, like a lethargic bat. A good look at a Serin reveals a remarkably small, short bill, a reflection of its diet, which consists of very small weed seeds. It usually forages on the ground for these but also feeds from herbs such as nettles. It additionally has a penchant for flowers, catkins and buds, and will munch these up contentedly in the branches of a tree. Its comfort with human habitats shows in the fact that it often nests in gardens.

This is a very small finch with a large head and minute bill. It is agile and restless. **ADULT** Washed a delicious yellow-green, with a bright yellow rump, but lacks the bold markings of other finches. Its yellow-green wing-bars are present but not obvious. It is heavily streaked over

minute bill

yellow with dark streaks

most of the body. **MALE** Lemon-yellow head, with broad stripe over eye. **FEMALE** Less yellow on head. **JUVENILE** Duller version of female. **VOICE** Song is a wonderfully effervescent, rushed phrase that sounds just like the tinkling of a bunch of small keys being shaken, or glass shattering. Distinctive jingling call. **MIGRATION** Mainly resident, but some French birds move south to Spain.

 BREEDING April–July, usually two broods. **NEST** In a bush or tree at varying height – a neat cup of plant stems and roots, with feathers and plant down for lining, built by female. **EGGS** 3–4 (rather few for a small bird), incubated for 13 days. **YOUNG** Leave nest after 14 days, but are dependent on parents for a week after.

ABOVE: *MALE*

BELOW: *FEMALE*

 The Serin feeds its young on regurgitated seed paste.

 The song of the male Serin directly stimulates females to put more effort into nestbuilding.

 Serins have greatly favoured song-posts, which can be shared by up to six individual males – like a stage.

FACT FILE

FAMILY Fringillidae (Finches). SIZE Length 11–12cm. FOOD Seeds, buds, flowers and invertebrates. SIMILAR SPECIES Siskin (p. 148) and Greenfinch (p. 144).

REDPOLL

Acanthis flammea

Fairly common in birch woodland and scrub; visits gardens mainly in winter.

This is not a common garden bird, but it does visit feeders from time to time. It also joins flocks of Siskins (p. 148), so check these out if you have them regularly. A very easily overlooked finch, the Redpoll lacks much of the colour of most other finches, especially in the wing-bars, which range from buff to dull white. Only in spring, when the male has a gorgeous raspberry-coloured throat and breast, might you say 'wow'. The red on the forehead is always easy to miss. Redpolls are also relatively quiet birds, lacking the liveliness of, for example, Goldfinches (p. 146). They are sociable, though, appearing in flocks. Redpolls pose an identification problem by being highly variable, and used to be split into different species. Their overall plumage varies from dull brown to almost snowy-white, and Redpolls also differ in size, with far northern birds being larger and fluffier.

This is an essentially small, streaky brown finch that feeds in trees. It is Blue Tit sized (p. 68), with a notched tail and very small bill. **ADULT** Occurs in varieties from tiny and rich brown (Lesser Redpoll, Britain

FACT FILE

FAMILY Fringillidae (Finches). SIZE Length 11–14cm. FOOD Mainly small seeds. SIMILAR SPECIES Linnet and Siskin. The Linnet (*Linaria cannabina*) is mainly a bird of fields and hedgerows, and only visits gardens near these. It occasionally visits feeders but is more likely to forage on herbs and on the ground. It has a grey bill and small white wing-bar.

buff wing-bars

raspberry-red forehead

and near continent, south Sweden) to plumper and frosty white (Common Redpoll, the north). The wing-bars are buff or white, not yellow (as in most other garden finches). Look for yellow bill, raspberry-coloured forehead and black bib. **MALE** Always some rich raspberry bleeding on to breast. **FEMALE** No raspberry colour on underparts, only on forehead. **VOICE** Song is a mixture of calls rarely heard in a garden. Call is a distinctive metallic *ji-ji-jit* ... **MIGRATION** Northern populations move south in variable numbers depending on birch crop (further if crop is poor).

 BREEDING March–July, rarely in gardens; 1–2 broods depending on the supply of seeds. **NEST** In a bush or tree, and lets down the finch clan by being a right mess, an untidy cup of twigs and grass, lined with feathers and plant down so the inside appears white. **EGGS** 4–6, incubated for 10–13 days. **YOUNG** Leave nest at 11–14 days but take another three weeks to become independent.

★ Redpolls may start breeding before the snow has melted in northern regions, even at temperatures of -20°C.

| JAN | FEB | MAR | APR | MAY | JUN | JUL | AUG | SEP | OCT | NOV | DEC |

YELLOWHAMMER

Emberiza citrinella

Fairly common in open country and hedgerows.

It is only rural gardens that attract the Yellowhammer, which is not a common visitor. However, if you get one you will probably get more, since it is very sociable, especially in winter, and it will join flocks of other species such as Reed Buntings (p. 156) and sparrows. If it does visit a garden, it is only likely to feed on the ground, or possibly on a tray feeder. It is a popular bird because not many of our species have its intense yellow colour, which is most obvious on the head of a male. Birds cannot synthesize yellow pigments, so they have to get the raw materials from insects such as caterpillars that have ingested plant juices, which involves effort; the yellower a Yellowhammer, the more attractive it will be to the opposite sex. Besides its colouration, the Yellowhammer is famous for its song, one of the few you can hear all summer long.

This is quite a big songbird with a long tail. It feeds on the ground but has an upright stance when perched. **ADULT** Always has a wash of mustard-yellow, from the bright to the subtle. Look for the unique

buttery yellow on head and breast

chestnut rump

chestnut rump and white outer-tail feathers. **MALE** Always has lots of yellow on the head. **FEMALE** Less yellow on the head, which is stripier. **VOICE** Song is a distinctive phrase endlessly repeated, even in the summer months. It is a dry rattle that usually has an emphatic ending, sounding as though the bird has run out of breath and is gasping at the end. In Britain it is rendered as 'A little bit of bread and no cheese'. Call is an emphatic *zit*. **MIGRATION** Mainly resident.

 BREEDING April–September, but most birds are late starters, in late May; there is often a second brood in July. **NEST** Cup of grass and moss placed on the ground, usually under a bush in a hedgerow. **EGGS** 3–5, incubated for 12–14 days. **YOUNG** Leave nest at 11–13 days, not yet able to fly. They are fed on insects.

On a long midsummer day, a Yellowhammer may sing 7,000 times.

FACT FILE

FAMILY Emberizidae (Buntings). SIZE Length 16–17cm. FOOD Range of small seeds from weeds; in summer, insects. SIMILAR SPECIES House Sparrow (female, p. 127) and Reed Bunting (female, p. 157). The Cirl Bunting (*Emberiza cirlus*) is a garden bird in parts of France. It has strong head-stripes and, in the male, a black throat; it also has a greenish, not chestnut, rump.

| JAN | FEB | MAR | APR | MAY | JUN | JUL | AUG | SEP | OCT | NOV | DEC |

REED BUNTING

Emberiza schoeniclus

Common in marshes and wet areas; locally visits gardens in winter.

This is an unusual garden visitor that can easily be mistaken for a sparrow. It sometimes joins flocks of other seed-eating birds on the ground, but seldom if ever uses hanging feeders. It will also only visit gardens in winter, because for the rest of the year it is a wetland bird. In winter it eats seeds, but unlike most finches, in summer its diet switches to invertebrates, which it also catches on the ground. A careful look soon reveals some subtle characteristics that set it apart. One is that is constantly flicks its tail, both when perched on a bush or tree, and on the ground. Another is that it is quiet, only calling sparingly and not cheeping endlessly like a sparrow. It is sociable in winter, so

black head

streaked, sparrow-like plumage

white collar and moustache

white outer tail feathers

FACT FILE

FAMILY Emberizidae (Buntings). SIZE Length 14–16cm. FOOD Seeds in autumn and winter; invertebrates at other times. SIMILAR SPECIES Sparrows, especially female House Sparrow (p. 127), and female Yellowhammer (p. 155).

if you have one Reed Bunting in the garden, you might well have several.

In appearance, the species is sparrow-like, but with a smaller head and longer, jerky tail. **ADULT** Note the white outer-tail feathers – no other streaky common garden bird has them. The stripy head and back are helpful for recognition purposes, too. **MALE** Handsome, with black head, white collar and white stripe down from bill, as if dribbling. Less black on head in winter. **FEMALE** Pale moustache-stripe down from bill. **VOICE** Song is a series of short, jerky phrases, often well spaced and rendered 'Three ... blind ... mice'. Call is a piercing *tseeu*, like a sharp intake of breath. **MIGRATION** Mainly resident, making local movements, but Scandinavian birds move south in winter.

ABOVE: *FEMALE (NOTE PALE MOUSTACHIAL STREAK)*

BELOW: *MALE IN SPRING*

BREEDING April–July, up to two broods, not in gardens but in wetlands. **NEST** Cup of grass and moss, sometimes reeds, usually placed on the ground by a tussock. **EGGS** 4–5, incubated for 12–15 days by female with some help from male. **YOUNG** Fed on insects and leave nest after only 9–12 days, some time before they can fly.

You can tell the marital status of a Reed Bunting by its song. If it has three elements with pauses between, the male is paired; if it is up to five notes delivered in rushed manner, it is single.

FURTHER READING

Bibliography

Cramp *et al.* 1977–94. *The Birds of the Western Palearctic*. Oxford University Press.

Holden, P. & Gregory, R. 2021. *RSPB Handbook of British Birds*. Fifth edition. Bloomsbury Wildlife.

Hume, R. *et al.* 2021. *Europe's Birds: An Identification Guide*. WildGuides. Princeton University Press.

Keller. V. *et al.* 2020. *European Breeding Bird Atlas 2*. Lynx Edicions.

Martin, G. 2021. *Bird Senses*. Pelagic Publishing.

Svensson, L. *et al.* 2022. *Collins Bird Guide*. Third edition. William Collins.

Thomas, A. 2019. *RSPB Guide to Birdsong*. Bloomsbury Wildlife.

Wernham, C. *et al.* 2002. *The Migration Atlas*. BTO/T & AD Poyser.

Websites

www.birdlife.org
https://birdsoftheworld.org
www.birdwatching.co.uk (magazine)
www.birdwords.co.uk (Dominic Couzens)
www.carlbovis.com

Storing your Sightings

Birdtrack (UK)
  www.bto.org/our-science/projects/birdtrack
eBird (Global): ebird.org

Societies

BirdLife Estonia: www.eoy.ee/EN
BirdLife Finland: www.birdlife.fi
BirdLife Norge (Norway): www.birdlife.no
BirdLife Sverige (Sweden): birdlife.se
BirdWatch Ireland: birdwatchireland.ie
British Trust for Ornithology (BTO): bto.org
Dansk Ornitologisk Forening (Denmark): www.dof.dk
Fuglavernd (Iceland): fuglavernd.is
Latvian Ornithological Society (LOB): www.lob.lv
Ligue de la Protection des Oiseaux (France):
  www.lpo.fr
Lithanian Ornithological Society (LOD): Birdlife.lt
Natagora (Belgium): www.natagora.be
Nature and Biodiversity Conservation Union
  (Germany): www.nabu.de
natur&ëmwelt (Luxembourg): www.naturemwelt.lu
Natuurpunt (Belgium): www.natuurpunt.be
Polish Society for the Protection of Birds: otop.org.pl
Royal Society for the Protection of Birds (RSPB):
  www.rspb.org.uk
The Wildlife Trusts: www.wildlifetrusts.org
Vogelbescherming Nederland:
  www.vogelbescherming.nl

Surveys

Many countries run surveys, including those for garden birds. In the UK they are:
• Big Garden Birdwatch (RSPB, see above) (January)
• Garden BirdWatch (BTO see above) (all year)

INDEX

Tick boxes are included next to the English name of each species so you can mark off species that you have seen.

Acknowledgements

Dominic Couzens wishes to thank John Beaufoy for agreeing to do the book, Rosemary Wilkinson for getting it all together, Nigel Partridge for the design and Krystyna Mayer for editing. What a great team. And much love to my wife, Carolyn, for coping with me while I wrote it - never easy.

Carl Bovis also wishes to thank John Beaufoy, and the production and editorial team. He'd like to thank his partner and three daughters for coping with him always having his camera with him on any family trip, and thank you to his Twitter followers, without whom he'd never have had the opportunity to be involved in the book.